ANTARCTICA
CRUISING GUIDE

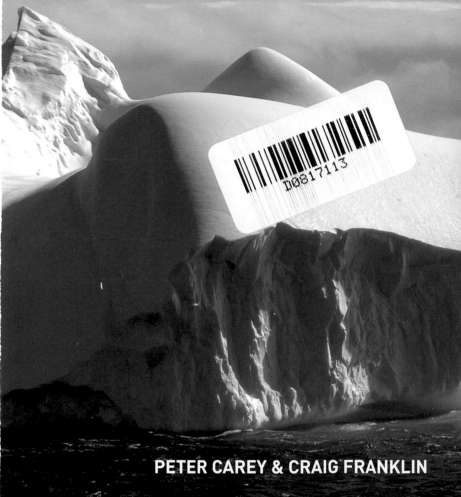

PETER CAREY & CRAIG FRANKLIN

For Gabriela and Noel

Second edition published in 2009 by Awa Press,
16 Walter Street, Wellington, New Zealand; this printing 2011.

First edition published in 2006.

National Library of New Zealand Cataloguing-in-Publication Data
Carey, Peter W. (Peter Wright), 1960-
Antarctica cruising guide / Peter Carey and Craig Franklin. 2nd
ed.
ISBN 978-0-9582916-3-7
1. Animals—Antarctica. 2. Antarctica—Description and travel.
I. Franklin, Craig E. (Craig Edwin) II. Title.
919.8904—dc 22

This book is typeset in Garamond and Din

Designed and typeset by Athena Sommerfeld
Printed by Midas Printing International Ltd, China

www.awapress.com

Front cover photograph: Gentoo penguins at Waterboat Point
Back cover photographs, clockwise from top left:
Antarctic tern, Adélie penguins, minke whale, Weddell seal,
black-browed albatross and chick, and gentoo penguin.

Map 1–Antarctica

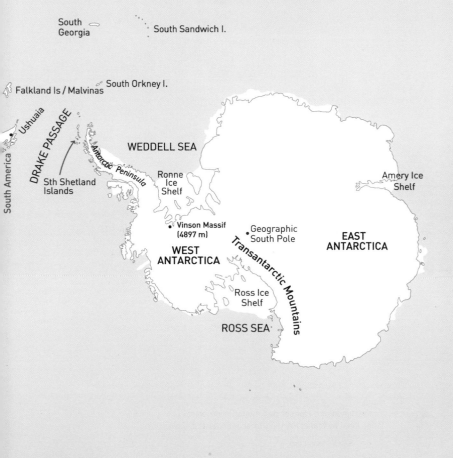

South Georgia

South Sandwich I.

Falkland Is / Malvinas

South Orkney I.

Ushuaia

South America

DRAKE PASSAGE

Sth Shetland Islands

Antarctic Peninsula

WEDDELL SEA

Ronne Ice Shelf

Amery Ice Shelf

Vinson Massif (4897 m)

Geographic South Pole

EAST ANTARCTICA

WEST ANTARCTICA

Transantarctic Mountains

Ross Ice Shelf

ROSS SEA

0	600	1200	kilometres
0	400	800	miles

Macquarie I. (Australia)

Campbell I. (NZ)

Auckland Is (NZ)

Tasmania (Australia)

Stewart I. (NZ)

Map 2–Antarctic Peninsula

Elephant I.

South Shetland Islands

Nelson I.   King George I.

Robert I.

Greenwich I.

Livingston I.

Smith I.   Deception I.

d'Urville I.

Antarctic Sound

Joinville I.

Dunde

Paulet

Low I.   Bransfield Strait

Palmer Archipelago

Brabant I.

Gerlache Strait

James Ross I.

Anvers I.

Graham Land

ANTARCTIC PENINSULA

Renard I.

Larsen 'B' Ice Shelf

Weddell Sea

Antarctic Circle

Larsen 'C' Ice Shelf

0	50	100	kilometres
0	20	40	60	miles

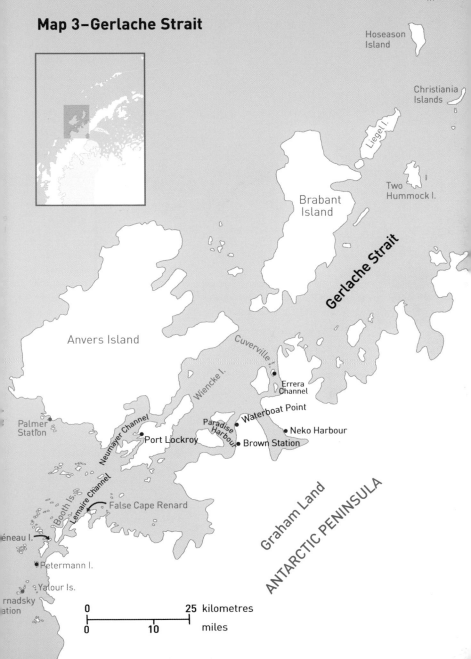

Map 3–Gerlache Strait

Hoseason Island

Christiania Islands

Liege I.

Two Hummock I.

Brabant Island

Gerlache Strait

Anvers Island

Cuverville I.

Errera Channel

Wiencke I.

Waterboat Point

Palmer Station

Paradise Harbour

Neko Harbour

Neumayer Channel

Port Lockroy

Brown Station

Booth Is.

Lemaire Channel

False Cape Renard

Graham Land

ANTARCTIC PENINSULA

éneau I.

Petermann I.

Yalour Is.

rnadsky ation

0			25 kilometres
0	10		miles

iv

Map 4–South Shetlands

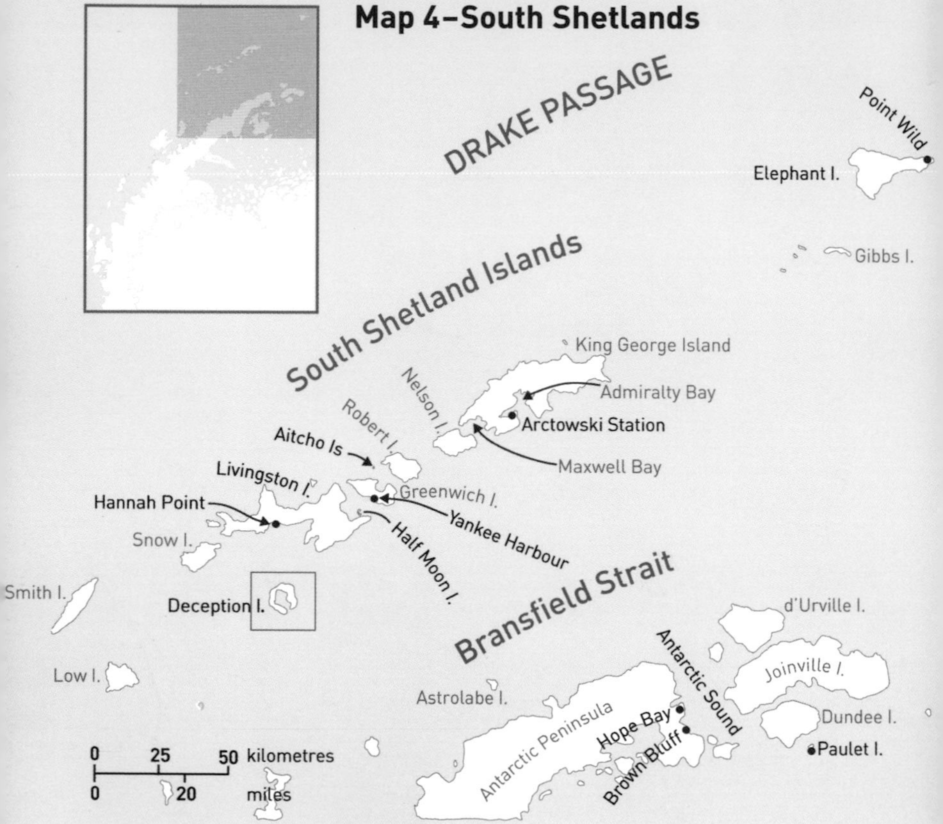

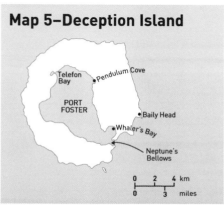

DRAKE PASSAGE

Point Wild

Elephant I.

Gibbs I.

South Shetland Islands

King George Island

Admiralty Bay

Nelson I.

Arctowski Station

Robert I.

Maxwell Bay

Aitcho Is

Livingston I.

Greenwich I.

Hannah Point

Yankee Harbour

Snow I.

Half Moon I.

Smith I.

Deception I.

Bransfield Strait

d'Urville I.

Low I.

Joinville I.

Astrolabe I.

Antarctic Sound

Dundee I.

Hope Bay

Paulet I.

Antarctic Peninsula

Brown Bluff

0   25   50 kilometres
0   20 miles

Map 5–Deception Island

Telefon Bay

Pendulum Cove

PORT FOSTER

Baily Head

Whaler's Bay

Neptune's Bellows

0   2   4 km
0   3   miles

Map 6–Ross Sea

Cape Adare

Possession Is.

VICTORIA LAND

Cape Washington

Ross Sea

Transantarctic Range

Franklin I.

Ross Island

Ross Ice Shelf

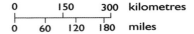

| 0 | 150 | 300 | kilometres |

| 0 | 60 | 120 | 180 | miles |

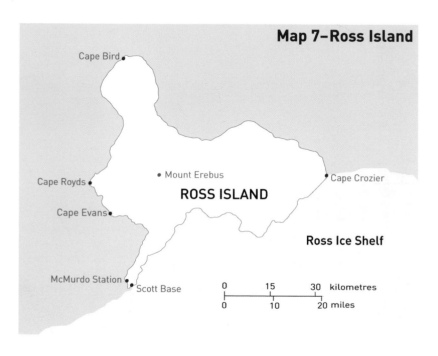

Map 7–Ross Island

Cape Bird

Cape Royds

Cape Evans

• Mount Erebus

ROSS ISLAND

Cape Crozier

Ross Ice Shelf

McMurdo Station

Scott Base

| 0 | 15 | 30 | kilometres |
| 0 | 10 | 20 | miles |

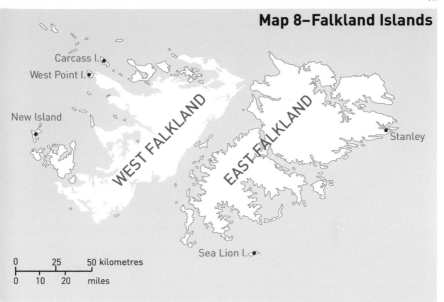

Map 8–Falkland Islands

Carcass I.
West Point I.
New Island
WEST FALKLAND
EAST FALKLAND
Stanley
Sea Lion I.

0   25   50 kilometres
0 10 20 miles

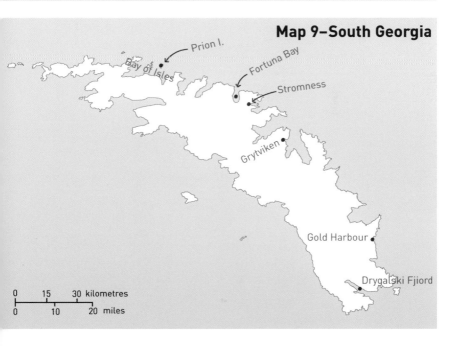

Map 9–South Georgia

Prion I.
Bay of Isles
Fortuna Bay
Stromness
Grytviken
Gold Harbour
Drygalski Fjiord

0   15   30 kilometres
0   10   20 miles

Contents

About the authors   02
Foreword   03

INTRODUCING ANTARCTICA 04
The frozen continent 07
Physical Antarctica 10
Importance of latitude 12
Big ice 13
Geology 22
Political Antarctica 21

PLACES 24
Ushuaia 26
Drake Passage 28
South Shetland Islands 30
Point Wild, Elephant Island 32
Deception Island 34
Whaler's Bay, Deception Island 38
Baily Head, Deception Island 42
Pendulum Cove, Deception Island 44
Half Moon Island 46
Hannah Point, Livingston Island 50
King George Island 54
Arctowski Station, King George Island 56
Yankee Harbour, Greenwich Island 58
Aitcho Islands 60
Antarctic Peninsula 62
Antarctic Sound 64
Hope Bay 66
Brown Bluff 68
Paulet Island 70
Cuverville Island 72
Paradise Harbour 74
Waterboat Point, Paradise Harbour 76
Brown Station, Paradise Harbour 80
Neumayer Channel 82

Lemaire Channel 84
Port Lockroy 86
Neko Harbour 88
Petermann Island 90
Gerlache Strait 92
Ross Sea **94**
Cape Adare 96
Cape Evans 100
Cape Royds 104
McMurdo Station / Scott Base 108
Ross Ice Shelf 112
Falklands Islands **114**
South Georgia **124**

LIFE IN ANTARCTICA 134
The terrestrial ecosystem **137**
Plants 138
Land-based animals 140
The marine ecosystem **141**
The Southern Ocean 141
The marine food web 144
Plankton 146
Sea-floor-dwelling organisms 148
Fish 149
Other vertebrates 149

BIRDS 150
Sea birds **152**
Black-browed albatross 158
Grey-headed albatross 160
Light-mantled sooty albatross 162
Royal albatross 164
Wandering albatross 166
Antarctic petrel 168
Cape petrel 170
Snow petrel 172

Southern giant petrel 174
White-chinned petrel 176
Wilson's storm petrel 178
Sooty shearwater 180
Southern fulmar 182
Antarctic prion 184
Antarctic shag 186
Kelp gull 188
Skua 190
Antarctic tern 192
Snowy sheathbill 194
Penguins **196**
Adélie penguin 202
Chinstrap penguin 206
Emperor penguin 208
King penguin 210
Gentoo penguin 214
Macaroni penguin 216
Rockhopper penguin 218
Magellanic penguin 220

MAMMALS **222**
Seals **224**
Antarctic fur seal 230
Crabeater seal 232
Leopard seal 234
Southern elephant seal 236
Ross seal 238
Weddell seal 240
Whales **242**
Blue whale 250
Fin whale 252
Humpback whale 254
Killer whale 256
Minke whale 258

THREATS TO ANTARCTIC CONSERVATION **260**

The Antarctic Treaty 262

Conservation **263**

Sealing 264

Whaling 265

Fishing 266

Invasion of alien species 267

Ozone depletion 267

Global warming 269

Conservation status of wildlife 272

Guidelines for Visitors 275

Glossary 279

Photograph credits 283

Acknowledgements 284

Index 286

About the authors

Peter Carey, Ph.D.

Peter Carey is a zoologist who has made more than 70 trips to Antarctica, including research expeditions as a scientist with the New Zealand Antarctic Programme and the Australian National Antarctic Research Expedition. He has also worked as a lecturer and expedition leader on a variety of Antarctic cruise ships. In the course of conducting research on such varying topics as penguin behaviour, sea-bird ecology, fish physiology and the social behaviour of seals, Peter has acquired a broad knowledge of the far south and the life that inhabits this frozen continent. He continues to visit Antarctica each summer, and is also working to ecologically restore a group of small islands in the Falklands archipelago. As the director of the SubAntarctic Foundation for Ecosystems Research (SAFER), a non-profit conservation organisation, he is actively involved in improving the wildlife habitat of these islands.

Craig Franklin, Ph.D.

Craig Franklin is a professor in zoology at The University of Queensland, Australia, and an Australian professorial research fellow. He has made more than 30 trips to Antarctica, including ten research expeditions as part of the New Zealand Antarctic Programme. Craig has published over 150 scientific works, including papers in the journals *Nature* and *Science*. His research programme focuses on how animals such as fish, frogs and crocodiles can survive and function in extreme and hostile environments and under challenging conditions. His current work in Antarctica is examining the impact of temperature increases on the physiology and survival of fish and other marine life. Craig is a strong proponent of wildlife conservation and spends his annual holidays lecturing on cruise boats about the Antarctic ecosystem and its spectacular wildlife.

Foreword

Antarctica is a big place to cover in a small book, and this is by no means a complete look at all things in the far south. Rather, it is a primer to the wonders of Antarctica, and a handy reference for when you want to identify that bird pecking at the ropes of your Zodiac, or know what to expect if you are landing at, say, Cuverville Island. Most of the book covers the Antarctic Peninsula, that mountainous finger of land that curls up from the South Pole towards South America. If your trip starts in Argentina, Chile or the Falkland Islands (and more than 95 percent do), this is the part of Antarctica you will be enjoying. Lucky for you, not only is the peninsula conveniently close to civilisation, it is also home to Antarctica's greatest wildlife diversity and some of its most spectacular scenery.

In this expanded second edition we have added two South Atlantic stepping stones to the Antarctic – the Falkland Islands and South Georgia – and the wilder, more remote Ross Sea region of Antarctica, most often visited from New Zealand or Australia.

The two main sections of the book describe the wildlife and the landing destinations. With wildlife, we've focussed on the species most commonly seen by the sea-borne passenger. Whether you're looking from the ship's deck or sloshing through penguin guano after landing from a tiny yacht, the birds and mammals described are the ones you're most likely to encounter. Similarly, we've chosen the landing sites visited most frequently, and by the greatest number of ships. The descriptions are designed to acquaint you with what to expect onshore at each spot, without taking away the thrill of making your own personal discoveries as you stroll, sit or stare at your next slice of paradise.

To present the most accurate information available, wherever possible we have used primary sources – that is, peer-reviewed scientific journals and texts, rather than websites and other non-academic sources. For stories about recent Antarctic history and anecdotes, we have spoken to people with firsthand knowledge of the events, rather than relying on rumour or the oft-told 'guides' tales'.

It is our hope that this book will help you to better understand and appreciate the beauty and charm of Antarctica and, in doing so, lead you to care for its future. Have a pleasant journey.

Peter Carey and Craig Franklin

Introducing
Antarctica

ANTARCTICA FACTS AND FIGURES

Size of the continent: **11.9 million sq km (4.59 million sq miles)**

Size of the Southern Ocean: **36 million sq km (13.9 million sq miles)**

Average thickness of Antarctic ice sheet: **2300 m (7546 ft)**

Maximum thickness of ice: **4776 m (15,670 ft)**

Highest mountain, Vinson Massif: **4897 m (16,066 ft)**

Average rainfall: **150 mm (6 in) per year**

Area of sea ice in summer: **4 million sq km (1.5 million sq miles)**

Area of sea ice in winter: **19 million sq km (7.3 million sq miles)**

Lowest recorded temperature: **−89°C (−128.2°F)**

Maximum wind speeds: **300+ km/h (186+ miles/h)**

Tourists visiting per year in 2009–10: **36,875**

Number of Antarctic Treaty nations in 2011: **48**

Number of scientific personnel present in summer: **4460**

Number of scientific personnel present in winter: **1094**

Number of scientific bases in 2011: **78**

The frozen continent

Antarctica, the only continent without a permanent human population, can be defined several ways.

Physically, Antarctica is a continent, the fifth largest. Sprawling across the South Pole and covering the most southerly latitudes, its northernmost point on the mainland is about 63°S. Transfer Antarctica to the northern hemisphere and it would be as if the continent stretched south from the North Pole to about Anchorage, Alaska, or Oslo, Norway. The land area covers nearly 12 million sq km (4.59 million sq miles). All but about 0.4 percent of this land is covered in a thick cloak of glacial ice, with only a few small ice-free areas, and spiky peaks protruding through the glaze.

Biologically, the boundaries of Antarctica extend far beyond the coasts of the continent, and its ecosystems are intrinsically linked to the Southern Ocean. The seas surrounding the land mass isolate the continent from the rest of the world's oceans and keep its temperature low. Located between 56°S and 60°S is the Antarctic Convergence, a fluctuating line where the cold waters of the Southern Ocean meet but don't mingle with the relatively warm waters of the subantarctic. This is the northern limit of 'biological' Antarctica. Many marine organisms are confined to one side of this barrier or the other.

Politically, Antarctica is covered by an international agreement, the Antarctic Treaty System, which includes all land south of 60°S. The treaty governs the actions of people visiting Antarctica, providing a code of conduct that aims to protect the continent's environment and wildlife (see pages 275–77).

introducing Antarctica

Paradise Harbour

PHYSICAL ANTARCTICA

Our fascination with Antarctica is largely tied to its icy strangeness. It is like nowhere else on Earth. The ice that makes Antarctica so exotic is, of course, tied to the continent's position at the bottom of the globe. However, Antarctica has not always been so far south. Had you been able to visit the continent 260 million years ago, you would have found temperate forests and lush vegetation. About 150 million years ago, dinosaurs roamed. Diversity such as this requires a warm climate – and this Antarctica had, as it was then located much closer to the equator.

Geologists now understand that the continents we see today have not always been in their current locations. Instead, over millions of years, moving at a rate that would keep pace with your growing fingernails, the continents have been shifting and drifting, floating on a liquid mantle of molten rock. Antarctica, South America, Africa, Australia and New Zealand are all just fragments of a large supercontinent we call Gondwana.

Transantarctic Mountain Range

The various pieces of this enormous land mass began to drift apart about 180 million years ago, beginning Antarctica's long slow trip from the near-tropics to a position as far south as you can go. At that time, today's 'Antarctica' was a series of fragments drifting separately. The largest of these is now known as East Antarctica, because it is found mostly in the eastern hemisphere. What is now called West Antarctica (which includes the Antarctic Peninsula) is made up of about five different fragments of Gondwana. East and West Antarctica are separated by the Transantarctic Mountain Range (see Map 1 at the front of the book).

The mountainous spine that is the Antarctic Peninsula used to be connected to the bottom of South America, until a spreading sea-floor zone rifted the two land masses apart. This moved the peninsula south toward East Antarctica and opened up the Drake Passage, placing an oceanic barrier between Antarctica and the rest of the world. This final split from other land-forms took place about 25 million years ago and set the stage for Antarctica to cool dramatically.

IMPORTANCE OF LATITUDE

Over the course of a year, all points on the Earth receive about the same amount of sunlight. What differs is the timing of this sunlight and the strength it has when it reaches the ground. Latitude – that is, your position in relation to the equator or the poles – is important. Near the equator, the length of a day in January is the same as in July – about 12 hours – and so sunlight quota is fairly evenly divided over the course of a year.

Moreover, the sunlight that strikes the Earth near the equator is quite strong because it is cutting through the Earth's atmosphere almost vertically and is therefore subject to less filtering. There is little seasonality, and the temperature is warm all year round. One hundred and eighty million years ago, Antarctica would have had conditions like this and supported a much wider array of plants and animals than it does today.

When you get close to the North Pole or South Pole, there is a marked difference during the year in the length of the day. In January, when the southern hemisphere is tilted towards the sun, land near the South Pole receives 24 hours of sunlight in a day: the sun literally circles above you and never approaches the horizon. At the exact South Pole, the sun sets once a year and rises once a year. The sunrise takes several days to be completed and takes place around September 21 (the vernal equinox), while the sunset takes place over several days near March 21 (the autumnal equinox). In July, when the tilt is reversed and the northern hemisphere is closest to the sun, the deep south receives zero hours of sunlight each day. This makes for a very cold half-year. Even in summer, the sun's rays come in at a low angle and have to penetrate such a thick layer of atmosphere they are robbed of much of their energy.

Being far from the equator, therefore, means little heat reaches the ground, which leads to a cool Antarctica. Historically, the rate of cooling would have accelerated when ice began to accumulate on the continent. Ice, being clean and white, tends to reflect 90 percent of sunlight back into the atmosphere, and this leads to even less heat being retained in the ground. The result is that an icy place gets cooler faster than a place with no ice. Put another way, it takes a huge increase in the amount of heat coming in to get rid of a glacier.

Eroded iceberg, Paradise Harbour

BIG ICE

The volume and variety of ice in Antarctica is one of the continent's defining characteristics. Visitors cannot help but be moved by the beauty of the icebergs, ice floes, ice sheets and ice shelves. There are two different kinds of ice: freshwater ice and sea ice.

Freshwater ice

All the ice on land in Antarctica is made up of fresh water. Precipitation that falls as snow (and almost all of Antarctica's moisture falls as snow) seldom melts in the cold conditions and so it piles up on top of the flakes from the last snowfall. The weight of snowfall on snowfall compresses the flakes, and over the course of several years the snow turns to little granulated balls called **firn**. After a further few years of snow accumulation, the firn becomes ice. This process happens all over the Antarctic continent and results in the build-up of glaciers and ice sheets.

When a body of ice starts to move downhill under its own weight, it is a **glacier**. In more temperate parts of the world, glaciers are confined to valleys in mountains. They flow slowly down their well-defined courses, and this makes it easy to appreciate them as rivers

of ice. Antarctica's glaciers, by contrast, are not confined to valleys, but are so deep and massive they fill the lowlands and spill over the tops of mountain ranges, blanketing the land on a grand scale.

Together these glaciers comprise a massive shroud of ice called an **ice sheet**. Also known as the Polar Plateau, this sets Antarctica apart from the rest of the glaciated world. Even the Greenland Ice Sheet, the only other such ice pile in the world, is dwarfed. The Antarctic

Ice Sheet covers the land and slowly pours off the edge of the continent, forming **ice cliffs** (left) where it meets the Southern Ocean. Most of the coast of Antarctica is made up of these ice cliffs, particularly on the Indian Ocean side where the underlying land is not high. On the mountainous Antarctic Peninsula, the ice cliffs are in many places broken by jagged peaks.

On average, Antarctica does not receive much precipitation, and most of what it does receive falls as snow. Meteorologists measure annual precipitation in its water equivalent: as a rough average, 10 mm of snow is the equivalent of 1 mm of water. Taken as an average over the whole continent, Antarctica receives only about 150 mm (6 in) of precipitation each year, which is far less than any other continent. However, the little bit that does fall tends to be preserved in the glaciers and so, little by little, the ice sheet has grown to its present size. At interior sites such as the geographic south pole or Russia's Vostok Station, less than 50 mm (2 in) falls each year.

The Antarctic Peninsula is the wettest part of the continent and often gets over 700 mm (27 in) of precipitation – about 7 m (23 ft) of snow each year. Early summer visitors to some sites often find themselves contending with waist-deep snow as they explore. In the summer months, the peninsula and other northerly coastal locations are warm enough for some precipitation to fall as rain.

The ice sheet covers Antarctica to a depth of up to 4776 m (15,670 ft). The weight of all this ice is so great it depresses the land underneath, and in many parts of the continent the base rock is below sea level. If you removed all the ice, you would find that Antarctica was not a single land mass but a series of large islands. The largest of these islands is in the area south of the Indian Ocean known as East Antarctica. This is where the ice sheet is thickest.

West Antarctica, the portion of the continent that lies south of South America, is much more mountainous, with peaks up to 4897 m (16,066 ft) protruding through the ice.

The ice sheet, essentially a gigantic, continental-scale glacier, flows downhill towards the coasts. Its rate of flow varies with the underlying terrain and other factors. In some places, there are 'ice streams' where the ice moves as fast as 2.2 m (7 ft) a day, while just a short distance away the ice crawls at a 'normal' glacial pace – about 10 times more slowly. On the Antarctic Peninsula, the ice visible from a cruise ship is not nearly as thick as the continental ice sheet that blankets the interior. What you can see are the many glaciers that have their 'headwaters' on the inland ice sheet, but which are now making the short, steep run to the sea. There are so many of these glaciers that most are without names.

Where glaciers or ice sheets meet the sea, they are subject to the destructive forces of wave action, tides and the relative warmth of liquid water. All of these conspire to weaken the ice, so that eventually pieces of the glacier break off and fall into the ocean. These pieces, the spawn of glaciers, are **icebergs**. Now free-floating, these immense packages of former snowflakes drift around at the whim of ocean currents and wind, delighting tourists and scaring ships' captains. With their myriad shapes and varying hues of white and blue, icebergs are truly one of the highlights of any Antarctic cruise.

In a few areas, the ice sheet pours down to the sea and does not break off right at the coast. Instead, it continues to flow forward, often coalescing with other glaciers until an enormous tongue of ice advances across the surface of the water. These **ice shelves** are unique to the polar regions. The crucial difference between an ice shelf and an ice sheet is that ice shelves are floating on the sea.

Anywhere you have an accumulation of ice, its surface will mimic the shape of the substrate underneath. Because ice shelves sit on the level surface of the sea, the top of an ice shelf is flat. The largest icebergs in the world (some the size of Belgium or Connecticut) are those that break off from the leading edge of ice shelves. These are called

tabular icebergs because of their flat, table-top profile. Icebergs of this size are too big to be pushed by wind or mere ocean currents. Instead, they are pushed forward in short bursts by the wave of water that sloshes around the globe with the fluctuating tide.

Glacier ice is formed under a lot more pressure than the ice you take from your freezer, or that which forms on a puddle in winter. This immense pressure, from the weight of consecutive snowfalls for thousands of years, is enough to squeeze out much of the air that is trapped between ice crystals. Thus, glacier ice takes a long time to melt, and the air that is still inside, because it is pressurised, tends to 'pop' when the ice does finally melt. If you get a chance to sit near the sea with lots of little pieces of glacier ice in it, you will hear the constant snapping and crackling of trapped air escaping.

The **air in ice** is also important in determining the ice's colour. Ice itself is actually blue, but it will seldom look that way unless you are looking at a large piece of glacier ice. So the real question is not 'why is ice blue?' but 'why doesn't it look blue all the time?' The answer is that, because our eyes aren't particularly sensitive instruments, we need a large chunk of ice to reflect back enough blue light for us to recognise it. Glacial ice is usually big enough; ice in your drinks is not.

However, some icebergs look white, and that is because we are seeing more than just ice: we are also seeing air bubbles. When light shines through ice that has a lot of air in it, the air reflects back all the colours of the spectrum, which we perceive as white. In the presence of a lot of ice reflecting its true blue, and a little bit of air reflecting its true white, the white prevails. The bluest ice you'll see is often from the bottom of a glacier, because that is where the oldest ice sits. The older the ice, the greater the pressure, and the fewer the air bubbles.

Some icebergs are black, and these take their colour from the rocks and gravel bound up within the ice. This **dirty ice** comes from the edges of the glacier, where it has been in contact with the land. Dirty ice is sometimes mistaken for ice with a seal on it, so look carefully at dark ice. Very rarely, too, you will see **green icebergs**, and these are so coloured because of algae bound up within the ice.

Bergy bits, the remnants of icebergs

Ice forms

- **Icebergs** are defined as being at least 5 m (16.5 ft) above sea level, so much of what we call an iceberg is in fact the next size down: a bergy bit.

- **Bergy bits** stand between 1 and 5 m (3.2 to 8.2 ft) above the waves.

- Ice less than 1 metre in height is a **growler** (from the sound made by these chunks as they ground along the sides of a wooden ship).

- Smaller still is **brash ice**. These little pieces, some no bigger than a hamster, are the ones that crackle the most as they melt in the surrounding sea water.

Brash ice

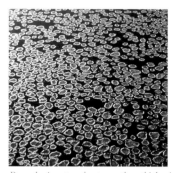 

Pancake ice at early stages, then thickening

Sea ice

While icebergs and their kin are made of fresh water, the ocean also freezes, forming sea ice. Every winter the sea around Antarctica freezes, and every summer most of this new ice melts again.

This pulse of freeze/melt has a huge impact on the flora and fauna of the Southern Ocean (see pages 141–43), and almost doubles the size of Antarctica, adding an additional 19 million sq km (11.8 million sq miles) of solid substrate to the region.

Ice floes surround tabular iceberg, Amundsen Sea

Only the surface freezes – to a depth of about 2 m (6.5 ft) – but this is thick enough to thwart the passage of all ships except true ice-breakers. It is also strong enough to allow bulldozers to be driven on it, or even large airplanes to be landed.

Because of its salt content, sea water freezes at –1.9°C/28°F. The process begins in autumn, when the temperature drops and a slush-like **grease (or frazil) ice** forms on the surface of the sea. As this consolidates, it clumps into little pancake-shaped pads, rounded at the edges where wave action has bumped them into their neighbours. As this **pancake ice** grows and solidifies, it becomes known as **pack ice**. Pack ice, which is actually composed of many **ice floes** – large pieces of floating ice – or smaller pieces, drifts around with the wind and currents and is an important habitat for seals and penguins.

Where the sea freezes but is attached to land in a solid sheet, this sheet is called **fast ice**. This form of sea ice is generally made up of huge sheets, and in contrast to the dynamic pack ice it is very stable and relatively seamless; it is on fast ice that aircraft are landed. The outer edge of the fast ice, where it meets the open sea or less stable pack ice, is essentially a de facto coastline. Penguins and seals will often rest here between meals, or to escape the predations of killer whales or leopard seals.

Ship's path through thin sea ice near Petermann Island

GEOLOGY

The rocks that lie under Antarctica's ice are varied and complex. As the continent was formerly connected to south-east Africa, eastern India, southern Australia, western New Zealand and southern South America, it is not surprising that Antarctic rocks show great similarity to those of these regions.

The rocks along the spine of the peninsula are mostly hardened **igneous (volcanic) rocks** that in many places have been subsequently deformed, folded and heated (metamorphosed) to their present condition. On the eastern margins of the peninsula lie **sedimentary rocks**, laid down by the river-borne silts and sands that eroded out of the mountains in warmer times. It is in these eastern sedimentary rocks that many of Antarctica's fossils have been discovered, including various molluscs, ammonites and brachiopods. Fossil remains of plesiosaurs (a marine reptile), sharks, turtles, penguins, whales and even a primitive possum have also been found in the complex rocks of the Antarctic Peninsula, with Seymour Island and Hope Bay being among the best-known sites for such discoveries.

Valuable minerals such as gold and silver are known to be present in Antarctica, but not in quantities that would attract mining activity, even if it were permitted. (Mineral extraction is presently prohibited by the Environmental Protocol of the Antarctic Treaty.) Oil deposits have also been found, particularly offshore, but no efforts have been made to extract them. Many experienced Antarctic workers believe it is just a matter of time before economic pressure increases and we see a real test of the agreement that currently bans the exploitation of oil and minerals in Antarctica.

Volcanic rocks, Half Moon Island

Amundsen-Scott South Pole Station of the United States. In the foreground are the flags of the 12 original signatory nations to the Antarctic Treaty.

POLITICAL ANTARCTICA

Unique among the world's land masses, Antarctica has no indigenous people, no permanent inhabitants and is not the sovereign territory of any nation. But it does have politics. Since 1961 it has been governed by an international agreement known as the Antarctic Treaty System, which sets aside the far south as an area for peaceful, scientific endeavours. It is a system that has worked remarkably well.

The treaty came about as a way to deal with territorial claims made by seven nations. During the first half of the twentieth century, Norway, Australia, France, New Zealand, Chile, Argentina and the United Kingdom all declared portions of Antarctica to be their own sovereign territory. The trickiest part was that Chile, Argentina and the United Kingdom claimed the Antarctic Peninsula, and each of these nations treated the other two as if they were trespassing. In some of the testiest situations, warning shots were fired over the heads of 'trespassers'.

The Antarctic Treaty dealt with these conflicting claims by ignoring them. It does not dissolve any territory claims, but nor does it recognise any of them. It merely gets on with the job of governing the continent as a large science laboratory, and more recently a tourists' playground. Military build-ups are banned, as is the disposal of nuclear waste. Every nation operating there has the right to inspect any other nation's facilities. The exchange of expertise and personnel has been a feature of the treaty; even during the worst of the Cold War, collaboration occurred between the USSR and the USA. Neither the USA nor Russia, which 'inherited' the Soviet interests, has made a territorial claim, although both have reserved the right to do so.

Chile's Eduardo Frei and Russia's Bellingbausen base buildings

With territorial claims off the agenda, Antarctic nations turned in earnest to science. Research stations were built by all 12 of the original treaty countries, and then by other nations as they acceded to the treaty. There are now stations of 29 different countries in Antarctica. But despite science now being the ostensible reason for being in Antarctica, many nations have kept an eye on the territorial prize. Should the Antarctic Treaty expire (it can now be dissolved by consensus), the claims game will be played again with serious intent.

The seven countries with existing territorial claims – Argentina, Australia, Chile, France, New Zealand, Norway and the United Kingdom – have maintained their presence in the areas claimed, and have set up bases, post offices and schools in an attempt to strengthen their claims. A few Chilean and Argentinian women have even been sent down to give birth to children in their claim areas so as to 'colonise' Antarctica.

The USA and the USSR (and, since its breakup, Russia) have also maintained a massive presence in Antarctica, especially in the 1960s, 1970s and 1980s, with each making sure they have a station within each separate claim area. The Soviets accomplished this by ringing the continent's coast with so many stations that, should the treaty expire, they could be said to have had as much right to be there as the claimant state. The USA achieved the same effect by placing a station at the geographic south pole, the point where six of the seven territorial claims intersect; Norway's claim is the only one that is not a 'piece of pie' extending all the way to the pole. Despite all this manoeuvring, science has always been the public face of national Antarctic programmes, and lots of valuable research has not only been accomplished but shared between signatory nations.

In the five decades since the Antarctic Treaty was originally signed, a further 36 countries have joined the club. The current total is now 48, so that 74 percent of the world's population is bound by the agreement. Further regulations have been added over the years to cover legislative needs not foreseen in the original document. The most significant of these is the Madrid Environmental Protocol, which came into force in 1998. The protocol spells out protection measures for the wildlife and environment, and details matters of waste disposal and environmental impact assessment. It sets the mandatory rules that govern all human activities in Antarctica. It also requires signatory nations to enact domestic legislation to enforce these rules for their citizens. Thus, citizens of a country that has signed the Antarctic Treaty can be punished at home if they disturb the environment in Antarctica.

The protocol also established the requirement that all people visiting Antarctica must get a permit to do so from the Antarctic authorities of their home nation. Gone are the days of launching an expedition and merely battling the elements. Now the first fight is with bureaucracy. Permits for those travelling to Antarctica on cruise ships are organised by the tour operator, but those on smaller private boats need to make their own applications.

Until the 1980s, scientists and their support personnel had the continent pretty much to themselves. A few hardy tourists came on small ships for a quick peek, but they could be measured in the hundreds. Not any more. By the mid 1990s, tourists outnumbered scientists and the disparity is increasing. In 2009, the winter population of scientists and staff was about 1094, rising to over 4460 in summer. In contrast, nearly 37,000 tourists visited Antarctica in the summer of 2009–10. Only 1155 (3%) of these tourists were citizens of non-Antarctic Treaty nations. The Environmental Protocol sets out guidelines by which all visitors (tourists, scientists, and support staff) must abide. With increased visitor pressure, it is important that these commonsense regulations are followed. (See Guidelines for Visitors, pages 275–77.)

Places

More than 90 percent of all Antarctic visitors begin or end their cruise in this charming city in southern Argentina. Nestled on the southern slopes of the tail end of the Andes, this is an excellent place to make last-minute preparations, or to splurge on 'civilised' luxuries upon your return from the ice. Ushuaia sells itself as the southernmost city in the world, and until recently that was true. However, Puerto Williams, 46 km (28 miles) south-east on the Chilean side of the Beagle Channel, has grown beyond its simple naval-base roots, and now holds this distinction: it is 13.8 km (8.6 miles) closer to the South Pole.

The land along the Beagle Channel was originally inhabited by Yahgan Indians, a nomadic people who ranged by canoe throughout the islands at the bottom of South America. They frequented the site of the town, which takes its name from the Yahgan description 'the bay that opens to the east'. A permanent settlement did not exist until 1869, when a mission was built by England's South American Missionary Society. This was followed by the establishment of an Argentine settlement in 1884, but the dismal climate – windy, wet, and cold – failed to attract migrants from the sunny north, and Ushuaia remained a small outpost.

That all changed with the introduction of government tax incentives in the latter part of the twentieth century. These were offered to businesses and citizens in an effort to develop Tierra del Fuego, Argentina's southernmost province. Today Ushuaia is a vibrant, expanding community with one of the youngest median ages of any Argentine city. The company tax breaks and the jobs they created have seen the population skyrocket from 7171 in 1975 to 57,000 today. Manufacturing has shrunk since the mid 1990s, but tourism has continued the town's prosperity, with cruise ships in summer and skiing in winter keeping the economy in better shape than most of Argentina's other provinces.

places

GEOGRAPHIC LOCATION	POINTS OF INTEREST
54°48'S, 68°18'W	Modern city with urban amenities
	Mountain backdrop
	Beagle Channel

The Drake Passage is a lively body of water, and a rite of passage for Antarctic tourists. Named after Sir Francis Drake, it extends 645 km (400 miles) from Cape Horn, the southern tip of South America, to the northernmost tip of Antarctica and is infamous for having some of the roughest seas in the world. Many sailing ships of yesteryear fell victim to the treacherous conditions, which can include 10 m (33 ft) swells, blasting winds and icy waters. It is across this stretch of water that you must pass if sailing to Antarctica from South America.

The passage is the narrowest portion of the easterly flowing Antarctic Circumpolar Current, the only place where it is squeezed between land masses. When forcing itself through this bottleneck, the ocean current moves a phenomenal 130 million cubic m (170 million cubic yards) of water per second. Somewhere in the middle of your crossing, you will traverse the Polar Front, or Antarctic Convergence. This is an oceanographic feature that marks the boundary between the relatively warm subantarctic water in the north and the colder Antarctic waters from the south. These do not mix readily, and so you will notice the water temperature suddenly drop several degrees. This signals the true start of your Antarctic adventures.

While the passage often lives up to its reputation for roughness, it is not uncommon to find calm conditions ('Drake Lake') if you are lucky enough to enter the area between the low-pressure weather systems that lurk in these latitudes.

The Drake Passage is a paradise for sea birds. This is the place to look for the giants of the south: the albatrosses. If the conditions aren't too rough, wrap up in warm clothing and venture out to the back of your ship to see these masters of flight glide effortlessly back and forth across the stern.

places

GEOGRAPHIC LOCATION	POINTS OF INTEREST	WILDLIFE
60°S, 60°W	Huge swells & rough seas	Wandering albatross *166*
	Antarctic Convergence	Royal albatross *164*
	Seasick bags	Black-browed albatross *158*
	Cape Horn	Light-mantled sooty
	The ceiling above your bunk	albatross *162*
		Southern giant petrel *174*

This archipelago forms the northern rampart of Antarctica, and is the first land most people see when visiting the continent. Stretching more than 530 km (330 miles), the South Shetlands are largely composed of volcanic rock, and their spiky peaks are heavily glaciated. Merchant mariner and sealer William Smith is generally regarded to have discovered the islands in 1819; the following year he returned with Edward Bransfield of the Royal Navy to claim them for Great Britain. However, it is likely they had been encountered more than 200 years earlier – in 1598 – by a Dutch fleet led by Admiral Jacob Mahu. These sailors, who reached 64°S, reported a land 'burdened under ice and snow'.

The South Shetlands are home to the greatest biological diversity in Antarctica, and their northerly position has encouraged a parade of visitors – sealers, whalers, scientists and now tourists. The relative warmth around the archipelago, and proximity to the foul weather of the Drake Passage, induce cloudy, grey conditions. Precipitation is frequent, and in summer months often falls as rain. The islands are separated from the Antarctic continent by the Bransfield Strait.

South Shetland Islands

Wild by name and by nature, this small rocky outcrop is best known as the site where Frank Wild, second-in-command on Ernest Shackleton's *Endurance* expedition of 1914–16, looked after the welfare of 21 men while Shackleton and five others sailed off to look for help. Elephant Island is jagged and heavily glaciated, so the spot did not have much to commend it, apart from being solid underfoot. For 105 days, the men had to contend with hunger, thirst, bone-jarring cold and an uncertain fate. They lived in a makeshift hut constructed from two overturned boats, stone walls and sailcloth, and to make things even less comfortable were in the middle of a smelly penguin rookery. It was, however, the best place to be, as the penguins had been living on the only part of the coast here that does not get washed by waves.

Few tourists land at Point Wild. The rough seas make it hard to do so safely, and there is so little room ashore that any traffic would disturb the nesting chinstrap penguins. A Zodiac cruise shows the place off nicely. From the boats you can marvel at its tiny scale and imagine what it must have been like to have been forced to camp here for three months in the middle of winter. None of the Wild camp remains, but you will see a bust of Captain Luis Pardo, skipper of the Chilean ship *Yelcho,* which eventually came to rescue the men on 30 August 1916. This memorial was erected in 1988.

The sharp-eyed may spy a macaroni penguin nesting among the chinstraps, and some of the rocks along the shore will, on closer inspection, morph into Weddell seals. Although chinstrap penguins now crowd the place, at the time of the Wild camp gentoo penguins were dominant. Fortunately for the stranded men, this species stays in the area longer than the chinstraps, which in mid April 1916 were just departing to spend the winter at sea. The men were able to kill many gentoos and stock their pantry with meat for the coming winter.

places

GEOGRAPHIC LOCATION	POINTS OF INTEREST	WILDLIFE
61°06'S, 54°52'W	Historic site	Chinstrap penguin *206*
	Chinstrap penguin colony	Macaroni penguin (just a few) *216*
		Skua *190*
		Cape petrel *170*
		Snowy sheathbill *194*
		Antarctic fur seal *230*
		Weddell seal *240*

Neptune's Bellows, from above

This actively volcanic island has been at the forefront of human activities in Antarctica since its discovery in 1820. It has the distinction of having been, in 1829, the first Antarctic land mass to be accurately surveyed. It played an important role in the sealing and whaling industries, and was the site, in 1928, of the first powered flight in Antarctica. In 1944 it became home to one of the earliest science bases, and today is one of the sites most visited by tourists.

The horseshoe-shaped island gets its name from the fact that the presence of a harbour is deceptive: the island is, in fact, the rim of an old volcano. The blast that blew off the top of the mountain and left the subsequent caldera happened about 10,000 years ago. After ejecting huge quantites of magma, the chamber collapsed and left a deep basin that has since been flooded by sea water. Port Foster, as this basin is known, is about 160 m (525 feet) deep.

The island has erupted many times since its discovery, most recently in 1967, 1969 and 1970. These eruptions occurred from fissures and cones on the north and eastern parts, not from the centre of the caldera. Although they caused no casualties, the eruptions destroyed the scientific bases of Chile and the United Kingdom, and led to the evacuation of all personnel on the Chilean ship *Piloto Pardo*. A nearby Argentinian base survived as it was upwind of the eruption.

In early 1992, the island was rocked by increased seismic activity, with an increase in the temperature of the groundwater and some land deformation. However, no eruption occurred. The volcanic activity probably explains why only 57 percent of the island is covered by glaciers, when neighbouring islands are almost 100 percent glaciated. Mount Pond (539 m/1768 feet) is the highest point, but it is usually hidden in heavy cloud. →

places

GEOGRAPHIC LOCATION	POINTS OF INTEREST	WILDLIFE
62°57'S, 60°38'W	Volcanic caldera	Chinstrap penguin *206*
	Geothermal hot springs	Cape petrel *170*
	Scientific bases	Antarctic fur seal *230*
	Extensive moss beds	Weddell seal *240*

Chinstrap penguins nest on the western rampart of Neptune's Bellows

→ Sailing into the caldera through the gap in the island known as Neptune's Bellows is a dramatic event, with rocky walls close on the starboard side and wildlife to be seen on both sides. Chinstrap penguins nest in a small colony on the port side; look for their pink guano stains against the grey rock. Cape petrels can be seen nesting on ledges on the cliffs close to starboard.

Nine species of birds breed on Deception Island, including more than 140,000 pairs of chinstrap penguins. As with most Antarctica wildlife, their colonies are restricted to the outer coasts. The relatively calm inner waters are not popular with penguins, and only a few wandering individuals are seen on the shores within Port Foster.

More impressively, Deception Island is home to 18 species of plants – mosses, liverworts and lichens – found nowhere else in Antarctica. The warm ground and high precipitation make it as good a growing ground as you'll find this far south.

places

Chinstrap penguins

Whaler's Bay has always been the hub of human activity in the Antarctic Peninsula region and remains so today, with over 10,000 tourists visiting each year. The same features that made it a good place for whalers and sealers – a well-protected anchorage and ice-free shoreline – make it an easy stop. Located just inside Neptune's Bellows, the narrow entrance to Deception Island, Whaler's Bay is literally littered with history.

You can stroll around the remains of the Norwegian Hektor whaling station, which operated from 1912 to 1931, and see some of the relics of this once-busy industry, including boilers, oil tanks, houses and a floating dry dock. Mixed in with these structures are the remains of British Base B, which was built here in 1944 as part of secret wartime Operation Tabarin, designed to keep an eye on any possible enemy activity in the far south. The British moved into some of the old whaling buildings as well as constructing their own, including an aircraft hangar. One of their old tractors is still here, mired deeply in the ground. British scientists used the base until it was destroyed in 1969 by a mud flow, triggered by a volcanic eruption that also destroyed the runway and buried the whalers' cemetery, which held 35 graves and a memorial to ten men who died at sea.

Further relics can be found north-east of the station area, where the shoreline is strewn with pieces of barrels and the remains of boats once used to carry fresh water. This is the route to walk if viewing Neptune's Window, a narrow break in the wall of the volcano that allows you to look out to sea. The edges of the Window are very crumbly, so don't get too close. Note also that the cliffs to the south-east of the Window are prone to rockfall. →

places

GEOGRAPHIC LOCATION	POINTS OF INTEREST	WILDLIFE
62°59'S, 60°34'W	Derelict whaling station	Skua *190*
	Derelict British base	Kelp gull *188*
	Historic site	Antarctic tern *192*
	Geothermal springs	Cape petrel *170*
		Antarctic fur seal *230*
		Weddell seal *240*

Remains of British Base B

Whaler's Bay, from the crater rim

→ The shoreline here is sometimes steaming where geothermally heated fresh water runs off the beach and mixes with the cold water of the sea. If enough hot water is present, the water along the beach can be a comfortable temperature for swimming – really more like wallowing. However, the amount of hot water flowing off the island has diminished in recent years, so the conditions these days are often not conducive to wallowing comfortably. The use of shovels to dig a pool in the sand is not appropriate.

Antarctic fur seals and Weddell seals are frequently seen lounging on the beaches here, but they do not breed anywhere on the island.

Whaler's Bay is an Historic Site (HSM71). Because it is intensely visited, a management plan has been prepared and you should be aware of the restrictions in place. Please stay on the seaward side of the station and the waterboats, to avoid damaging the fragile fluvial plains that have formed inland. Don't enter any buildings, climb on boats or collect any 'souvenirs'. And if hiking to Neptune's Window, make the approach in a single file, along the existing track.

Antarctic fur seals, with remains of barrels used for whale oil

Officially known as Rancho Point, Baily Head is a popular site for lovers of chinstrap penguins and boisterous surf. The seas breaking on the steep beach are often too rough for a safe landing, but when conditions permit a visit here is very rewarding.

Many tens of thousands of chinstrap penguins nest on the scoria slopes in a natural amphitheatre close behind the beach. Their commute between nest and ocean requires them all to file through a narrow valley. An additional delight here is the presence of significant greenery, since the slopes are often bright with the glow of *Prasiola crispa*, a hardy annual alga.

If you want to explore this interior amphitheatre, be careful to keep to one side of the valley so you do not disrupt the flow of commuting penguins – you wouldn't want to delay the delivery of food to the chicks! Another great spot for penguin-watching is right at the beach, where you can be educated and entertained as the birds come and go in the breaking waves.

Exercise caution near any of the steeper slopes and cliffs, as huge boulders can drop off without warning. Fur seals haul out on to the beach here in the latter parts of the summer. As elsewhere, they should not be approached too closely: keep further away than 15 m (50 ft) to avoid frightening them.

places

GEOGRAPHIC LOCATION	POINTS OF INTEREST	WILDLIFE
62°58'S, 60°30'W	Chinstrap penguin colony	Chinstrap penguin *206*
		Skua *190*
		Antarctic fur seal *230*

Remains of Chile's Cerda base

Antarctic tern

Pendulum Cove is a barren patch on the inner shoreline of Deception Island. It is notable for its paucity of wildlife and for the tortured metallic remains of a former Chilean scientific station. The base, Presidente Pedro Aguirre Cerda, was destroyed in 1967 and 1969 by volcanic eruptions that occurred close by. One eruptive fissure headed towards the building in which the station staff were sheltering, cracked its walls and forced the occupants to flee. There was no loss of life and the 27 men escaped overland to the British base at Whaler's Bay. However the eruption grew in magnitude and after two hours began to engulf this base as well. Both Chileans and British staff were taken off the island by the Chilean ship *Piloto Pardo*.

Much of the station wreckage has been cleaned up and removed by the Chilean government, but the area is designated an Historic Site (HSM76).

Further uphill is a protected area (ASPA140g) which has been set aside to preserve the rare mosses that grow there. A permit is required for entry into this area, so it's best not to hike too far inland from the remains of the base.

The shoreline here sometimes provides good 'swimming' conditions when enough hot water flowing off the land mixes with the cold sea water in the bay. Look for areas of steaming beaches – if there's no steam, the swimming will be no fun at all. If attempting swimming, do not modify the landscape with shovels.

places

GEOGRAPHIC LOCATION	POINTS OF INTEREST	WILDLIFE
62°56'S, 60°36'W	Abandoned Chilean base Historic site Geothermal springs	Antarctic tern *192*

Weddell seal

Tucked in close to the towering glaciated shores of Livingston Island, the low-lying crescent of Half Moon Island is dwarfed to insignificance on approach. However, once you are close to the eastern-side anchorage, its jutting turrets of volcanic rock stand out starkly against the icy cliffs or, more often, the low cloud beyond.

Most of the wildlife is concentrated on the southern prong of the crescent. About 3300 pairs of nesting chinstrap penguins are the most obvious feature, but with binoculars it is also easy to watch the nesting activities of Antarctic terns, skuas and kelp gulls on prominent rocky ramparts. Stay away from these nesting areas to avoid disturbing the birds.

Wilson's storm petrels also breed on the island. Their nests are tucked into the spaces between the accumulated rocks on the talus slopes of the island's highest points, so they are best observed as they flit about looking as if they want to land but can't seem to find the right spot. A tiny number of black-bellied storm petrels breed here too, as do cape petrels. Do not climb the talus slopes as it is easy to unwittingly crush a storm petrel on its nest.

Weddell seals frequent the beaches, and you will often need to look carefully to differentiate them from the rocks on the snowy southern shore. By late January, Antarctic fur seals also begin to loiter on the beaches and may even climb up on to the plateau. Their numbers increase as the summer ends. In March, you may find the landing beaches crowded with more than a hundred of these furry beasts. →

places

GEOGRAPHIC LOCATION	POINTS OF INTEREST	WILDLIFE
62°36'S, 59°55'W	Argentinian base	Chinstrap penguin *206*
	Chinstrap penguin colony	Antarctic tern *192*
	Colourful lichens & mosses	Antarctic shag *186*
	Old wooden boat	Snowy sheathbill *194*
		Skua *190*
		Kelp gull *188*
		Wilson's storm petrel *178*
		Antarctic fur seal *230*
		Weddell seal *240*

Chinstrap penguin colony

→ There are two obvious man-made structures on Half Moon Island: an Argentinian station and a disintegrating wooden boat. Cámara Station is a summer-only base that traditionally supports about 20 staff. Much of the work involves basic tasks such as recording weather details and maintaining a presence, but Cámara Station was also the site of a number of tourist-impact studies in the 1990s. Most recently, it has been used by Argentinian ornithologists and geomorphologists – scientists who study the physical features of the Earth – while carrying out research.

As for the dilapidated wooden boat, there is no properly documented history for it, or for how it got here, although one experienced shipwright has identified the construction as being a style popular in the 1930s.

places

Southern elephant seals, during moult

Hannah Point has more biodiversity than most sites in Antarctica, but is also one of the most vulnerable to disturbance, since many of the species that breed in the narrow confines of this southward-projecting promontory are very skittish.

Visitor movements can do serious damage at this biologically rich site. Extreme care must be taken when ashore, particularly along the higher slopes and cliff edges where giant petrels nest. Give these ferocious-looking but easily spooked birds *at least* 50 m (165 ft) of space.

Chinstrap and gentoo penguins nest here in segregated colonies, and a few macaroni penguins may also be seen tucked in with the chinstrap groups, so for bird lovers there is much to enjoy.

Lovers of fat, loudly belching, smelly seals will also be enthralled. Southern elephant seals haul out and pile up on one another in muddy wallows during the annual moult, when they shed their fur along with their top layer of skin. The seals lose a lot of heat in the process, and like to huddle together to stay warm. Antarctic fur seals also frequent the shoreline. These agile animals should not be approached too closely. →

places

GEOGRAPHIC LOCATION	POINTS OF INTEREST	WILDLIFE
62°39′S, 60°37′W	Abundant wildlife	Gentoo penguin *214*
	Nesting penguins	Chinstrap penguin *206*
		Macaroni penguin *216*
		Snowy sheathbill *194*
		Skua *190*
		Kelp gull *188*
		Cape petrel *170*
		Antarctic shag *186*
		Antarctic tern *192*
		Southern giant petrel *174*
		Southern elephant seal *236*
		Antarctic fur seal *230*

Southern giant petrel

Antarctic fur seal

→ Much of the exposed rock in the South Shetland Islands is volcanic in origin, but Hannah Point is also home to some sedimentary rocks that are rich in fossilised leaves and wood. Please do not 'souvenir' anything during your visit here, or anywhere else in Antarctica.

Livingston Island is the second-largest of the South Shetland Islands, and is dominated by an icy interior with peaks up to 1770 m (5807 ft). It has a complicated shape, with six major peninsulas stretching for 73 km (45 miles) from east to west. Although the island was the base of many sealing operations in the early 1820s, it was not properly surveyed and mapped until 2005, when a Bulgarian team completed the difficult task.

Most tourist visits are confined to the southern coast, where underwater surveys are more complete. The north coast is treacherous and was the scene of several shipwrecks in sealing days, including the greatest loss of life in the history of Antarctica. This occurred in 1819 when the Spanish ship *San Telmo* foundered with the loss of 644 lives.

places

Macaroni penguin

The largest of the South Shetland Islands, King George is also home to the biggest collection of scientific stations in Antarctica. Eight different nations operate bases here, attracted by the relatively mild weather and ease of access, as well as the ability to share logistics. Maxwell Bay and Admiralty Bay, located on the more protected southern side, are home to most of the bases. The island is 69 km (43 miles) long and up to 25 km (16 miles) wide. The vast majority is glaciated, with only the tallest mountains poking through the mantle of ice, and some coastal areas exposed. The highest point reaches 679 m (2228 ft).

As with most of the Antarctic Peninsula, the earliest visitors were sealers. William Smith is credited with discovering the island in 1820, naming it after George III of England, although on a nearby island British sealers under Joseph Herring had already been sealing for more than a month. The numerous fur seals here were quickly the target of other entrepreneurs, and for the next three summers King George Island was awash with sealing gangs, until the animals were so scarce as to be no longer worth hunting.

King George Island may be the most 'civilised' place in Antarctica. Year-round stations are operated by Chile, Russia, China, South Korea, Poland, Brazil, Argentina and Uruguay. In Maxwell Bay, the Chinese, Russian and Chilean stations are close enough together to make an almost urban area. The Chileans operate an airstrip that takes many flights in support of the neighbouring nations, as well as some tourist traffic. However, generally poor weather and the limited amount of landing-aid instrumentation result in many flights being delayed for days at a time. This area is also the site of the Antarctica Marathon, a full 42 km (26 mile) course that attracts adventurous runners from around the world.

places

GEOGRAPHIC LOCATION	POINTS OF INTEREST	WILDLIFE
62°00'S, 58°15'W	Scientific bases	Gentoo penguin *214*
	Extensive wildlife	Adélie penguin *202*
	Dramatic scenery	Chinstrap penguin *206*
		Antarctic tern *192*
		Snowy sheathbill *194*
		Southern giant petrel *174*
		Southern elephant seal *236*

The low gravel shores in front of Poland's Arctowski Station are home to a wide variety of wildlife. Fur and elephant seals are commonly found lounging on the shore here. Some venture several hundred metres inland. Adélie, gentoo and chinstrap penguins all frequent the beach because they nest in abundance in the colonies on the nearby surrounding hills. These nesting areas are off-limits to all visitors as they are within Antarctic Specially Protected Area 128. Entry is by permit only. However, there are usually plenty of birds wandering outside the protected area.

The ground in front of the base is particularly verdant, with a thick carpet of the grass *Deschampsia antarctica*. Richly coloured lichens abound on the rocks.

The beach here is one of the best places for viewing whale bones, with the remains of several large baleen whales – skulls, ribs, jaws and other massive bones – in evidence. The bones are a reminder of one of the earliest industries in the Antarctic. Be careful walking along the beach as the loose cobble can be tough on ankles.

The station is named in honour of Henryk Arctowski, the geologist on Adrien de Gerlache's *Belgica* expedition of 1897–99, the first Antarctic expedition to focus on scientific research. The base is staffed year-round and is scientifically active. Station personnel have constructed a visitors' centre near the landing beach and sell a small selection of souvenirs. You can pay with US dollars, in cash.

places

GEOGRAPHIC LOCATION	POINTS OF INTEREST	WILDLIFE
62°10'S, 58°30'W	Polish scientific base	Adélie penguin *202*
	Adélie penguin colony	Chinstrap penguin *206*
	Lichens, mosses	Gentoo penguin *214*
	& hairgrass	Skua *190*
	Whale bones	Antarctic fur seal *230*
	Visitors' centre – souvenirs	Southern elephant seal *236*

The broad cobble beach of Yankee Harbour lies protected behind a long gravel spit that is often visited by resting seals. The bones of those that rested too long can be found strewn along this rocky finger of land.

A gentoo penguin colony lies on the higher ground to the east, although many birds seem to commute from across the spit, instead of swimming into the harbour itself. The penguins have taken over a dilapidated emergency refuge hut, built in 1953 from discarded packing cases.

The wide open, gently sloping plains of Yankee Harbour allow for good hiking without disturbing the wildlife. That said, be careful not to tread on the lichens and lush mosses to be found on the higher slopes beyond the penguin colony, and do not venture on to the crevassed glacier that overlooks the harbour.

Yankee Harbour gained its name from the frequent activity here of American sealers in the 1820s. The protected harbour was a safe haven for small ships (as it is today for modern yachts), and evidence of this historic activity is still present. Look for the try-pot on the beach at the base of the spit. This iron pot would have been used to boil seal blubber, releasing the valuable oil within. The oil was then stored in wooden casks and sold in the United States or Europe.

places

GEOGRAPHIC LOCATION	POINTS OF INTEREST	WILDLIFE
62°32'S, 59°47'W	Sealers' try-pot	Gentoo penguin *214*
	Good hiking	Skua *190*
	Gentoo penguin colony	Kelp gull *188*
		Wilson's storm petrel *178*
		Weddell seal *240*
		Southern elephant seal *236*
		Antarctic fur seal *230*

Weaner southern elephant seal

Named for the phonetic pronunciation of the letters H and O, as in Hydrographic Office, the Aitcho Islands form one of the most jagged pieces of coastal Antarctica. Their position in the relatively warm and damp South Shetland Islands permits the growth of luxurious beds of mosses, so hikers need to be careful not to damage the greenery: even one footprint on these fragile plants can destroy several years of growth.

The black volcanic islands are home to many species. A walk along some of the island's many small hills or black shores will yield excellent wildlife viewing.

Early in the summer, it is not unusual for people sitting quietly on the beach to be closely approached by one of the many recently weaned elephant seals looking for a meal. They are absolutely fearless and harmless as they look for someone from which to suckle. In fact, all the adult females will by this time have departed, so the weaners eventually get hungry enough to go to sea and feed themselves. You are not allowed to approach the seals, but if they approach you it's okay.

There are whale bones scattered along the length of the south-facing beach. These large bones are encrusted with colourful lichens, indicating the many decades they have been here.

places

GEOGRAPHIC LOCATION	POINTS OF INTEREST	WILDLIFE
62°24'S, 59°47'W	Weaner elephant seals	Gentoo penguin *214*
	Whale bones	Chinstrap penguin *206*
	Chinstrap penguin colony	Southern giant petrel *174*
	Colourful lichens & mosses	Snowy sheathbill *194*
	Gentoo penguin colony	Skua *190*
		Weddell seal *240*
		Antarctic fur seal *230*
		Kelp gull *188*
		Southern elephant seal *236*

This finger-like projection of the continent of Antarctica curls northward toward South America, and its spine of many mountains is often called an extension of the Andes. In a few spots, the peninsula is less than a few dozen kilometres in width. However, crossing it without flying is a difficult undertaking: the whole of the peninsula is covered in steep, glaciated mountains, deeply crevassed and with heavy snowfall. The western side is the wettest part of Antarctica and receives tens of metres of snow each year. The eastern side is much drier, since the moisture-rich winds empty themselves of snow and rain as they rise up over the mountains. Consequently, the Weddell Sea region enjoys many more blue skies than the murky grey conditions so prevalent in the west. In contrast with most of Antarctica, the Antarctic Peninsula has recently been warming two to three times faster than the rest of the world, and so has attracted a lot of attention from climatologists.

Antarctic Peninsula

Tabular iceberg

Adélie penguin

Antarctic Sound is a parking lot for giant icebergs. It lies tucked between the northernmost tip of the Antarctic mainland and the large glaciated islands of Joinville and Dundee. The sound takes its name not from its obvious location within the Antarctic, but from the ship *Antarctic* of the Swedish Antarctic Expedition of 1901–03, led by Otto Nordenskjöld, which was the first to sail through it.

Antarctic Sound is often whipped by strong winds that funnel through this gap between land-forms, or scream downhill from the polar ice-cap on the mainland. The latter are called katabatic winds. With the wind and currents that squeeze through here come icebergs from the ice shelves in the Weddell Sea. Hundreds of massive chunks drift into the sound, and because many are too deep for its shallow waters, they become grounded and may spend several years being buffeted by the waves and winds until they break up, tip over or float free – again as a result of wave and wind action.

This area has some of the best sightseeing in the entire peninsula. The myriad blues and whites and fantastic shapes can be appreciated from the comfort of your ship as it weaves its way through the icy seascape. Many of the icebergs are known as tabular bergs because their tops are as flat as tables. This kind of berg comes from an ice shelf, of which there are only a few in Antarctica, so they are an exotic treat to behold. Look out for Adélie penguins resting on some of the smaller ones.

In 2004, a submarine volcano was discovered in the eastern reaches of Antarctic Sound. Named Jun Jaegyu after a South Korean scientist who lost his life in the South Shetland Islands in 2003, the volcano has recently been active. Its summit is presently about 275 m (902 ft) beneath the ocean surface.

places

GEOGRAPHIC LOCATION	POINTS OF INTEREST	WILDLIFE
63°20'S, 56°45'W	Tabular icebergs	Adélie penguin *202*
		Southern giant petrel *174*
		Minke whale *258*
		Humpback whale *254*

Esperanza Station

Stone hut of Swedish expedition, 1903

Hope Bay, which is on the mainland of Antarctica, is home to a relatively large number of people – about 50 men, women and children. But an even larger number of Adélie penguins – more than 100,000 pairs – occupy its southern coast. The best landing sites for seeing these penguins are deep in the bay.

The people live at the mouth of the bay, in Argentina's largest Antarctic base, Esperanza. Established in 1951 and staffed by Argentinian army personnel, Esperanza is a year-round facility with the unusual feature of having entire families present, instead of just the scientific and support personnel found at most Antarctic stations. The families are at the base for a year at a time. In many ways the station is like a small village; it even has a proper school and a teacher. The first child to be born in Antarctica entered the world here in January 1978. Since then at least seven more children have been born at Esperanza.

The first human inhabitants of the bay were three Swedes, members of Otto Nordenskjöld's expedition, who were forced to spend the winter of 1903 here. After their attempt to rescue the main expedition further south was thwarted by bad ice conditions and their ship did not return for them, they constructed a small stone hut and endured a miserable winter eating penguins and seals. The remains of their hut, designated HSM39, are near the Argentinian landing jetty.

The British built their Base D in Hope Bay in 1944 and worked here, just a few hundred metres from the Argentinian station, until 1963. Base D, or Trinity House as it was known, was later used for the location filming of *Mr Forbush And The Penguins*, a 1971 film starring John Hurt and Hayley Mills, released in the United States as *Cry Of The Penguins*. In 1997 the restored building was given to Uruguay. It is now used by that country for research.

places

GEOGRAPHIC LOCATION	POINTS OF INTEREST	WILDLIFE
63°23'S, 57°00'W	Argentinian base	Adélie penguin *202*
	Adélie penguin colony	Skua *190*
	Historic site	Snowy sheathbill *194*
	Uruguayan base	

TOP *Adélie penguin colony*
ABOVE *Leopard seal*
RIGHT *Cape petrels*

Brown Bluff is on the mainland of Antarctica. As the name implies, the towering cliffs here are brown and abrupt, soaring to 745 m (2444 ft). With only a few hundreds metres' space between the vertical cliffs and the sea, they are a dramatic sight. The cliffs are the remnants of an ancient volcano, and the ice-cap behind them is hidden from view when you look up from the beach.

Although the space between cliff and sea is narrow, it is packed with wildlife. You can stroll among clumps of nesting gentoo and Adélie penguins, and observe the chicks of kelp gulls hiding between the rocks. Walking conditions near the beach are relatively easy as the gravel is not too rough, but be careful not to disrupt the flow of penguins that use the shoreline like a highway.

Cape petrels and snow petrels nest on the ledges of the cliffs; both species can be seen wheeling about prior to landing there. In a few places on the lower slopes, snow petrels' nests can be reached safely for a closer look – a rare opportunity to see these Antarctic icons on the nest – but take care not to disturb the birds.

As with any large penguin colony (there are around 20,000 pairs of Adélies and 600 pairs of gentoos), leopard seals are frequently seen patrolling the shoreline, particularly around the time the chicks are fledging.

places

GEOGRAPHIC LOCATION	POINTS OF INTEREST	WILDLIFE
63°32'S, 56°55'W	Adélie penguin colony	Gentoo penguin *214*
	Gentoo penguin colony	Adélie penguin *202*
		Skua *190*
		Kelp gull *188*
		Cape petrel *170*
		Snow petrel *172*
		Wilson's storm petrel *178*
		Leopard seal *234*

The tell-tale conical shape of volcanic Paulet Island in the northern Weddell Sea instantly informs the visitor of its geologic origins. On closer approach, the shape of the island is quickly ignored when the scale of the enormous Adélie penguin rookery is appreciated. More than 100,000 pairs of these penguins nest here. Their pinkish guano-stained areas become readily apparent on the beaches and well up the slopes. Antarctic shags also have a colony, and skuas nest on many of the high ridges.

Paulet Island was home to Carl Larsen and 17 of his crew from the *Antarctic*, the vessel supporting Swedish geologist Otto Nordenskjöld's 1901–03 expedition. The ship was crushed in the pack ice while trying to retrieve the parties at several points further south, and the men were lucky to scramble across the ice floes to Paulet Island. Here they spent the winter of 1903 in a stone hut, with penguins and the occasional seal to sustain them. One young sailor, Ole Wennersgaard, died; he is buried in a makeshift grave south of the hut. Nesting penguins make it impossible to access the grave, which, together with the remains of the hut, is a protected Antarctic Historical Site (HSM41).

Because of the large penguin colony on Paulet Island you will often see leopard seals feeding on penguins, particularly later in the summer when the chicks are fledging. Weddell seals are also frequent visitors to the island's gravel shoreline.

LEFT *Visitors mingle with Adélie penguins near the remains of Larsen's 1903 hut.*

places

GEOGRAPHIC LOCATION	POINTS OF INTEREST	WILDLIFE
63°35'S, 55°47'W	Adélie penguin colony	Adélie penguin *202*
	Historic site	Antarctic shag *186*
		Skua *190*
		Wilson's storm petrel *178*
		Leopard seal *234*
		Weddell seal *240*

Nestled in close to the Antarctic Peninsula mainland, dome-shaped Cuverville Island is visited frequently by cruise ships and adventurers. The northern shores support large colonies of gentoo penguins, while a cruise along the eastern coast reveals breeding kelp gulls and Antarctic shags.

The slopes of the high dome are luxuriantly dappled with many species of mosses and lichens, making this one of the most verdant places in this part of Antarctica. Hiking on the vegetated slopes should not be attempted, as the plants damage easily. Skuas are also found nesting on the higher reaches. The need to avoid disrupting their reproduction efforts is another good reason not to venture too high.

The relatively gentle slopes on the north and west sides of the island make Cuverville an easy place for small-boat landings. The island has played host to a number of adventurous recreational expeditions. It was also the base of operations for several summer-only parties from the Scott Polar Research Institute, who conducted research projects here in the mid 1990s. The island was named by de Gerlache on his 1897–99 *Belgica* Expedition and honours J.M.A. Cavelier de Cuverville, a French vice-admiral.

The relatively shallow waters between Cuverville and Rongé Islands are usually littered with icebergs that have drifted in and become stuck. If you are cruising this area in a Zodiac, look out for leopard seals or crabeater seals in the water or on icebergs. Weddell seals occasionally haul out on shore.

places

GEOGRAPHIC LOCATION	POINTS OF INTEREST	WILDLIFE
64°41'S, 62°38'W	Gentoo penguin colony	Gentoo penguin *214*
	Mosses & lichens	Antarctic shag *186*
		Skua *190*
		Kelp gull *188*

With a name like Paradise, a place has to be really spectacular to meet expectations. Paradise Harbour manages this feat even on a cloudy day. When the sun is shining, it is absolutely gorgeous.

Lying between the Antarctic mainland and Bryde and Lemaire Islands, the bay was named by early twentieth-century whalers who were not immune to its charms. Whales continue to visit, and minke, humpback and killer whales are all regularly seen here.

There are three channels into the bay, and when the tide is running the currents are strong enough to noticeably move icebergs. In most parts, the water is hundreds of metres deep, but there are a few spots for ships to anchor.

Most tour ships to the region will at least steam through here. Many will also do landings on some of the tiny pieces of bare rock that protrude through the jumbles of ice, which pours off the steep mountains that line the bay. Zodiac cruises through the recently calved bergy bits and loose, broken brash ice are also very popular.

places

GEOGRAPHIC LOCATION	POINTS OF INTEREST	WILDLIFE
64°51'S, 62°54'W	Spectacular scenery	Minke whale *258*
		Humpback whale *254*
		Killer whale *256*

The steep, glaciated slopes surrounding Paradise Harbour plunge directly into the sea in all but a few places. One of these rare ice-free spots is Waterboat Point at the northern entrance to the bay. This patch of exposed rock is home to several hundred pairs of gentoo penguins. It is also the site of a Chilean base.

The penguins were certainly here first. The sealers, whalers and explorers who were the earliest human visitors, and named this beautiful bay, noted their presence. A pioneering penguin study was carried out here from 1921 to 1922 by Maxime Charles Lester, a surveyor in his twenties, and his 19-year-old companion Thomas Bagshawe, a geologist. The men, who spent 12 months living in a makeshift camp, were the remnants of a four-member British expedition that had set out to map the Weddell Sea coast. The point takes its name from their use of a ruined waterboat, abandoned by whalers, as part of their winter dwelling.

The site of the mens' hut, just south of the base buildings and the main flagpole, is now covered by nesting penguins. Intriguingly, in Lester and Bagshawe's time the area was home to hundreds of chinstrap penguins, as well as gentoos. Now less than ten pairs of chinstraps remain.

Chile established its base at Waterboat Point in 1951, naming it Gonzalez Videla Station after the Chilean president who, in 1948, became the first head of state to visit Antarctica. At first the base was occupied year-round, with livestock kept to supply fresh meat and milk during the winter months. Straw can still be seen mixed in with the mud in a few places →

TOP LEFT *Gonzalez Videla station*
BOTTOM LEFT *Waterboat Point; sign in foreground marks site of historic hut*

places

GEOGRAPHIC LOCATION	POINTS OF INTEREST	WILDLIFE
64°49'S, 62°51'W	Gentoo breeding colony	Gentoo penguin *214*
	Chilean Antarctic base	Chinstrap penguin *206*
	Antarctic historic site	Antarctic shag *186*
		Weddell seal *240*
		Kelp gull *188*
		Snowy sheathbill *194*
		Skua *190*

→ The base was abandoned in 1964 but reopened in the mid 1990s and is now staffed, in summer only, by eight to 12 members of the Chilean Air Force. The staff operate a gift shop for visitors, and are developing a small museum in one of the original buildings. The peninsula on which the base stands is cut off from the mainland at high tides but, because it is more often connected than disconnected, Waterboat Point is still classified as a part of the continent of Antarctica.

Waterboat Point has at least three leucistic (white) penguins in residence. These unusual-looking birds are not true albinos because they have normal skin pigment. However, the feathers that would ordinarily be black are off-white or ivory-coloured. Leucistic birds will breed with 'normal'-coloured birds. It is not known if their striking colour leaves them more susceptible to predation. In addition to the penguins, kelp gulls, skuas and snowy sheathbills also make their homes here.

LEFT *Gentoo penguin and chick*

Antarctic shags

Brown Station is perched on a tiny bump of rock, backed by dramatic, icy slopes. The Argentinian summer-only station has rarely been occupied in recent years. It is the site of one of Antarctica's most enduring and intriguing stories. In 1984, when the station was occupied year-round, the station doctor, deciding that he couldn't face the prospect of the long winter ahead and knowing there were still some ships in the area, burnt the place to the ground. No one was injured, and all staff were evacuated and taken to the nearby United States base, Palmer Station, and thence back to Argentina.

Wildlife is not a major attraction here, although a few dozen gentoo penguins can be found nesting under some of the buildings and sheathbills breed in some rock clefts. Antarctic shags are more numerous, but they can be seen only from a ship or Zodiac because they occupy the cliffs to the west of the station. Just east of the station, Weddell seals often haul out on the gravel bars that are barely above sea level but covered with snow.

You can generally make good use of the small hill behind the base buildings by hiking to the top and sliding down the snowy slopes on your backside.

Brown Station was known as Almirante Brown until 2004, when Argentina dropped all military titles from the names of its stations.

This site is on the Antarctic mainland.

places

GEOGRAPHIC LOCATION	POINTS OF INTEREST	WILDLIFE
64°53'S, 62°52'W	Nesting Antarctic shags	Gentoo penguin
	Argentinian base	(only a few) *214*
		Snowy sheathbill *194*
		Antarctic shag *186*
		Kelp gull *188*
		Weddell seal *240*

Steep glaciers tumble directly into the sea along much of the length of this narrow fiord called the Neumayer Channel. The imposing bulk of Anvers Island forms the western side of the channel, while Doumer and Wiencke Islands are on the east. Port Lockroy is a bay within the channel.

The transit is a worthwhile detour, even for ships that are not headed for that landing site. While quite narrow in most places, the water is more than 200 m (656 ft) deep, and large ships can make the passage if the wind isn't blowing too hard. The channel is 26 km (16 miles) long and has a sharp bend that, from a distance, gives the impression of its having a dead end. Once in close, however, the rest of the channel opens out and an exit becomes obvious.

Neumayer Channel was first spotted in 1874 by the first German expedition to Antarctica, led by Eduard Dallmann, who had been commissioned by the Polar Shipping Corporation (*Polarschiffahrtsgesellschaft*) to investigate the potential for whaling and sealing. However, the channel was not explored until 1898, when Adrien de Gerlache and the *Belgica* arrived.

It was named in honour of Georg von Neumayer (1826–1909), a prominent German geophysicist who was a major force in organising Antarctic exploration and promoting international cooperation: he established the first International Polar Year (1882/83) and the first Antarctic Year (1901). Von Neumayer's name has also been attached to a mountain, a glacier, a cape and a set of cliffs, in quite widespread parts of Antarctica. These place names were chosen by explorers from Belgium, Germany, Great Britain and Sweden – a sign that von Neumayer's influence was not contained by national borders. The German polar research station also bears his name.

places

GEOGRAPHIC LOCATION	POINTS OF INTEREST	WILDLIFE
64°47'S, 63°30'W	Spectacular scenery	Whales *250–59*
		Crabeater seal (on ice floes) *232*

Perhaps the best-known fiord in Antarctica, Lemaire Channel cuts a path between the continent's mainland on the east and Booth Island in the west. It is almost 11 km (7 miles) long and renowned for its spectacular scenery, with near-vertical peaks rising close on both sides. Wandel Peak, on Booth Island, is 980 m (3215 ft) high. The channel is deep too, measuring about 150 m (492 ft) most of the way. Ice sometimes chokes it closed, so if you are lucky enough to make it through make a point of spending your time out on deck. Some of the tallest peaks are so high you can't appreciate them when looking through a window.

The current that flows through this passage is strong enough to drag in large icebergs that sometimes block traffic. The ice also provides excellent platforms for resting leopard and crabeater seals, so keep an eye out for dark objects. Humpback and minke whales are frequently spotted. Antarctic shags and gentoo penguins nest in small numbers in a couple of places. But really, Lemaire Channel is not about the wildlife; it's about a grand landscape that forces you to tilt your head back.

At the northern entrance, on False Cape Renard (actually an island), are two prominent pointy peaks known officially as Una's Peaks, and colloquially to Antarcticans as Una's Tits. They were so named by members of the Falkland Islands Dependencies Survey (forerunner of today's British Antarctic Survey) in honour of a secretary in the Governor's Office in Stanley, capital of the Falkland Islands, one of the last women they would see before sailing south.

The channel was first sighted in 1874 by the German whaler and sealer Eduard Dallmann, but it was named in 1898 by the Belgian Adrien de Gerlache for his country's famed African explorer, Charles Lemaire. An island in Paradise Harbour is also named after Lemaire.

places

GEOGRAPHIC LOCATION	POINTS OF INTEREST	WILDLIFE
65°04'S, 63°57'W	Spectacular scenery	Gentoo penguin *214*
		Antarctic shag *186*
		Crabeater seal (on ice floes) *232*
		Leopard seal *234*
		Minke whale *258*
		Humpback whale *254*

Port Lockroy
(includes Jougla Point and Goudier Island)

Nestled under the dramatic mountains of Wiencke Island, this sheltered bay is one of the most popular destinations for visitors to Antarctica. The port is really just a small bay, but it is so well protected that it is a favoured anchorage for many of the small yachts that sail to Antarctica each summer. The site's appeal to mariners was obvious from the earliest days of human exploration in the area, and a small whaling operation was headquartered here in the early 1900s. Some whale bones can be seen on the floor of the bay and ashore in the penguin colony on Jougla Point. The bones that make up a seemingly intact skeleton are from a number of different individuals and were 'reconstructed' by members of the United Kingdom Joint Services Expedition who visited the site in the 1970s. The spiky peaks to the south-east, reaching up to 1435 m (4708 ft), are the Fief Mountains.

The restored buildings of an early British scientific station stand on Goudier Island. Base A, as it was known, was built in 1944 as part of the secret Operation Tabarin, which saw British forces occupying strategic locations on the Antarctic Peninsula in order to detect any use of these areas by German naval forces. The Germans never showed up. Scientific staff took over the base in 1948 and it operated continuously until 1962. In 1996 the buildings were restored by members of the Antarctic Heritage Trust, and today Bransfield House is used as a museum, gift shop and post office. When the base was established, Goudier Island was attached to nearby Wiencke Island by a glacier, but this has since retreated sufficiently for the island now to stand alone in the harbour.

Early in the summer you can sometimes land on the fast ice that covers the bay in spring, allowing you to eschew Zodiacs and simply walk over to the penguin colonies or museum.

places

GEOGRAPHIC LOCATION	POINTS OF INTEREST	WILDLIFE
64°49'S, 63°30'W	British Antarctic base	Gentoo penguin *214*
	Whale bones	Antarctic shag *186*
	Gentoo penguin colony	Skua *190*
	Gift shop & post office	Snowy sheathbill *194*
		Weddell seal *240*
		Kelp gull *188*

Along the eastern side of Andvord Bay, the sheer ice cliffs that line the coast are broken by a tiny rocky point known as Neko Harbour. Bare ground is limited here; however, a small colony of gentoo penguins nests well up the slope from the beach. If you visit them when there's snow on the ground, try not to walk in the tracks used by the penguins: your footprints will make holes that will hinder the progress of these short-legged birds.

Even further up the hill you'll find nesting skuas. Be careful not to disturb them. If a skua is diving or screaming at you, you're too close to the nest and should retreat down the hill. Caution must also be used if hiking on to the glacier here, as crevasses are not always obvious. Those without the proper equipment should stick to *terra firma*.

Most parties land at Neko Harbour for the chance to walk on mainland Antarctica, and for the fantastic views of the ice cliffs nearby. However, extreme care must be taken when on the beach, as falling ice from the cliffs frequently sends waves washing over the shoreline. More than one group has had to rush uphill to avoid being knocked over or swept away.

Neko Harbour is named after the whaling factory ship that often operated in this bay between 1911 and 1924. The small wooden hut just above the beach is an emergency shelter built by the Argentinian Antarctic Programme.

TOP LEFT *Ice calving from the cliffs*
BOTTOM LEFT *Skua menacing gentoo colony*
BOTTOM RIGHT *Snowy sheathbill*

places

GEOGRAPHIC LOCATION	POINTS OF INTEREST	WILDLIFE
64°50'S, 62°33'W	Gentoo penguin colony	Gentoo penguin *214*
	Excellent ice-cliff viewing	Snowy sheathbill *194*
		Skua *190*
		Kelp gull *188*

Antarctic shag

Petermann Island is the southernmost of the popular landings in the Antarctic Peninsula. At a latitude of 65°10'S, it is about the equivalent of Fairbanks, Alaska, in the northern hemisphere. If your ship turns around here, you will have reached a point 2813 km (1748 miles) from the geographic south pole. The snow here is often deep, even late in the summer, so moving around can take some effort. Remember not to use the tracks employed by the commuting penguins: your deep footprints make it difficult for the penguins and their short legs. Gentoo penguins nest near the usual landing site, and they also cluster around a small Argentinian refuge hut that dates from 1955.

Human activity here goes back as far as 1874, when a German expedition led by Eduard Dallmann first visited the area. Dallmann named the island after August Petermann, a prominent geographer. In 1909, French explorer Jean-Baptiste Charcot and his men wintered here, squeezing their ship snugly into the tiny bay they called Port Circumcision (so named because it was discovered on 1 January, which in the Christian calendar is marked as the day when Christ was circumcised). The mooring points may be seen on the rocks. The only other evidence of their productive winter is the rock cairn on Megalestris Hill. Near the cairn, a cross has been erected as a memorial to three members of the British Antarctic Survey who lost their lives on the sea ice nearby in 1982. This historic area is designated HSM27.

Adélie penguins and Antarctic shags nest on the shores of the next bay to the north. Red and green snow algae are prolific on most of the slopes. It is safest to stick to the eastern side of the island, which will keep you off the glaciers which have hidden crevasses.

places

GEOGRAPHIC LOCATION	POINTS OF INTEREST	WILDLIFE
65°10'S, 64°10'W	Gentoo penguin colony	Adélie penguin *202*
	Adélie penguin colony	Gentoo penguin *214*
	Historic site	Snowy sheathbill *194*
	Memorial cross	Skua *190*
		Kelp gull *188*
		Wilson's storm petrel *178*
		Antarctic shag *186*

If there's one body of Antarctic water that nearly every cruise ship uses, it's the Gerlache Strait. This generous strait separates the large islands of Brabant and Anvers from the continental mainland, and most ships cross through it at least once, and often two or three times, as they zigzag between landing sites.

The strait is named after Adrien de Gerlache, leader of the *Belgica* expedition of 1897–99. The *Belgica*'s party of 19 men was the first to winter in the peninsula region, surviving for 13 months on board their ship after it became locked in ice south-west of here in March 1898. The expedition members were from many different countries, and language barriers contributed to an arduous time in the confines of the ship, especially from mid May when they were in virtual darkness 24 hours a day. For 32-year-old American Frederick Cook, who later falsely claimed to have scaled Mount McKinley (the highest mountain in North America) and been first to the Geographic North Pole, this was perhaps his finest hour. He was the doctor on board and one of the men who helped hold morale together. The third mate, Norwegian Roald Amundsen, later to distinguish himself as the most successful polar explorer, made his Antarctic debut here.

As straits go, the Gerlache is quite wide. The many beautiful islands and coastlines are not as close as in some other spots in Antarctica. Humpback whales are very frequently seen here. Attracted by the abundance of food, they migrate from the waters off Brazil to gorge themselves on krill all summer long. If you're keen to see whales on your trip to Antarctica, this is the one place you should make sure you keep watch for them out the window. Or, better yet, dress warmly and stand outside, where you can keep a sharp eye out for the dark back and bushy spout of a feeding humpback, or pods of fast-swimming minke and killer whales.

GEOGRAPHIC LOCATION	POINTS OF INTEREST	WILDLIFE
64°30'S, 62°20'W	Spectacular scenery	Humpback whale *254*
	Whales	Minke whale *258*
		Killer whale *256*

places

The Ross Sea is the southernmost part of the Southern Ocean, occupying the large dent in the Antarctic continent south of New Zealand. It is named for British admiral James Ross, who discovered it in 1841 while in command of the ships *Erebus* and *Terror*. Here ships can sail closer to the geographic south pole than they can anywhere else, with about 78°S accessible most summers. This is one of the ways the Ross Sea differs from the more commonly visited Antarctic Peninsula. It is also much colder, so sea ice can be a challenge to ships, even in summer.

A consequence of the harsher conditions is reduced biodiversity. For example, only two species of penguins – Adélie and emperor – live here, while the peninsula region is home to five. But there is an upside: despite the cold, there is a greater chance of clear skies. Precipitation is generally light, and almost never falls as rain.

Most ships need at least six days to reach the Ross Sea from the bottom of New Zealand, and at least four from subantarctic Macquarie Island. The vast distances and lack of human presence – in the 2008–09 season only 575 tourists visited the Ross Sea – give this region a unique appeal. You will seldom cross paths with another ship, nor see navigational aids along the shore. For those willing to embrace wildness and isolation, the Ross Sea is a rewarding destination.

Ross Sea

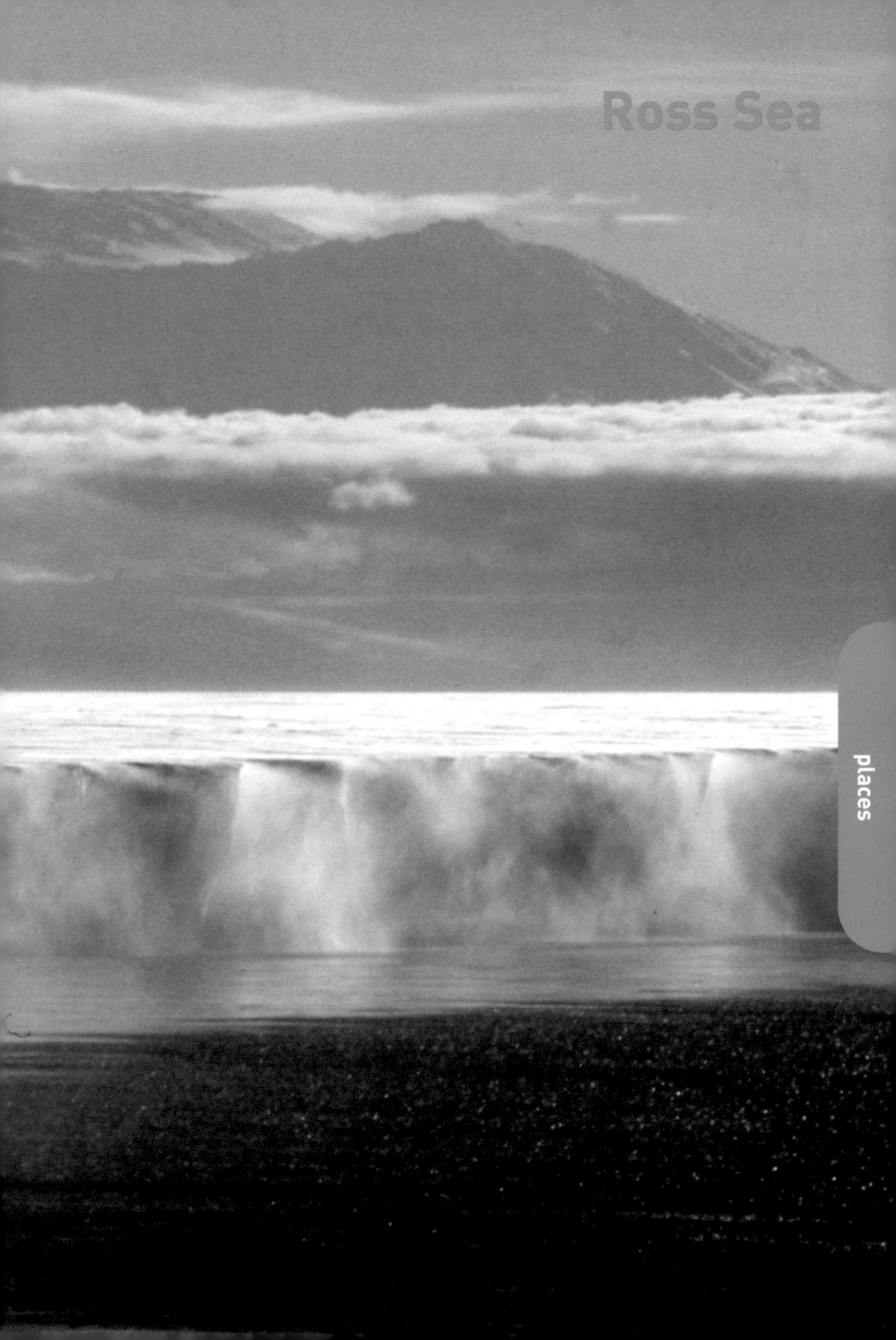

Borchgrevink's hut – the oldest building in Antarctica

Adélie penguin chicks

At the western entrance to the Ross Sea lies windswept Cape Adare, home to the oldest building in Antarctica and the world's largest Adélie penguin rookery. The stout little building is one of two that were erected in 1899 by members of the *Southern Cross* expedition led by Carsten Borchgrevink, and has stood up surprisingly well to more than a century of abuse by vicious Antarctic conditions. Borchgrevink's expedition was formally known as the British Antarctic Expedition because it was funded by a British philanthropist, but most of the members were Norwegian. It achieved a number of 'firsts': first to winter ashore in Antarctica; first to use sled dogs; first man to be buried on Antarctica.

The interior of the hut is fascinating, with personal touches not seen in the British huts further south. Lots of interesting grafitti adorns the bunk walls, including poems, mathematical calculations, and a delicately drawn portrait of a woman. In 1911, six members of Robert Scott's *Terra Nova* expedition spent the winter here, using Borchgrevink's two huts, as well as erecting one of their own. This 'Northern Party' hut was not built to the robust standards of the earlier structures, and is now quite dilapidated.

The hut and all its adjacent artefacts are a designated Historic Monument under the Antarctic Treaty system (HSM22). A permit and a certified guide are required for visits, and only four persons are allowed in the hut at a time. The area surrounding the huts is an Antarctic Specially Protected Area (ASPA159) and also requires a permit. Remember that penguins should not be disturbed; the presence of their nests may prevent access to some sites of historic interest. →

places

GEOGRAPHIC LOCATION	POINTS OF INTEREST	WILDLIFE
71°18'S, 170°12'E	Oldest building in Antarctica	Adélie penguin *202*
	Largest Adélie penguin rookery	Skua *190*
	First grave on Antarctica	

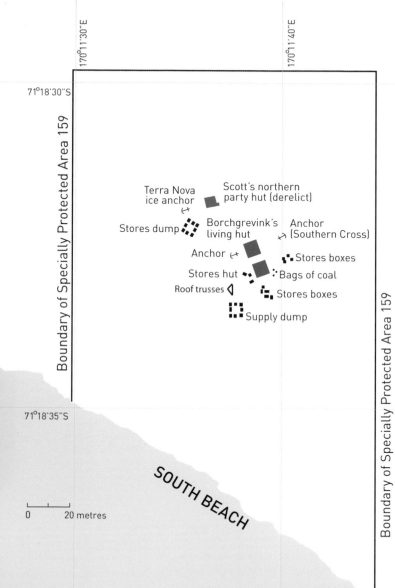

170°11'30"E

170°11'40"E

71°18'30"S

Boundary of Specially Protected Area 159

Terra Nova
ice anchor

Scott's northern
party hut (derelict)

Stores dump

Borchgrevink's
living hut

Anchor
(Southern Cross)

Anchor

Stores boxes

Stores hut

Bags of coal

Roof trusses

Stores boxes

Supply dump

Boundary of Specially Protected Area 159

71°18'35"S

SOUTH BEACH

0   20 metres

Cape Adare

→ These huts are surrounded by hundreds of thousands of Adélie penguins. The number of breeding pairs varies from year to year, from a maximum of 282,307 in 1986 to about 169,200 in 1990. South polar skuas also nest around the fringes of the colony.

The grave site of Nicolai Hanson, biologist on the Borchgrevink expedition, who died of unknown causes on October 14, 1899, is located on the hill well above the penguin colony. The grave is hard to find, and with nesting penguins now occupying the safest routes on the climb to the summit, visits are not recommended. Hanson signed his name on the wall of his bunk a month before he died.

The flat area with the huts and penguin colony is a moraine – glacier rubble – and is known as Ridley Beach; it was named by Borchgrevink after his mother's surname before marriage. The actual Cape Adare is the prominent cliff to the north. This was named in 1841 by Ross Sea discoverer James Ross for his friend and patron Viscount Adare.

places

Adélie penguin rookery

Cape Evans is a small ice-free corner of volcanic rock projecting into McMurdo Sound, and famous as the starting point for Robert Scott's fatal trip to the geographic south pole. The members of Scott's *Terra Nova* expedition (1910–13) made their headquarters here as it was the furthest south the ice would allow them to sail when they arrived in January 1911. The site is named for Lieutenant Edward Evans, who had been second in command on Scott's first Antarctic expedition, 1901–04. The prefabricated building the men erected still stands, thanks to the skilled work of a number of New Zealand historians, conservators and carpenters.

The building and surrounding area are an Historic Monument under the Antarctic Treaty system (HSM16); all visitors must adhere to the rules set out in the site management plan. It is also an Antarctic Specially Protected Area (ASPA155) for which an entry permit is needed. A maximum of 12 persons are allowed inside the hut at any one time. Visitors must be accompanied by a certified guide.

The hut and its environs are strewn with artefacts from the heroic era of Antarctic exploration. Around the rough wooden walls are shelves still stocked with cocoa and mustard powder, and the books and glassware give the visitor an excellent sense of what it was like to live here. The main table is still in place, as are Scott's quarters and the men's bunks. Many who visit claim that, while inside, they have the sense that Scott and his men have only just left.

By the 1950s, ice had built up inside the hut from snowdrift blown through cracks in the walls. When historians first excavated, they found the place as it had been left by its final occupants, the 1914–17 Imperial Trans-Antarctic Expedition. These men, who used the hut in dire circumstances only two years after the survivors of Scott's party had departed, created the tableau preserved in the ice. Two poignant →

places

GEOGRAPHIC LOCATION	POINTS OF INTEREST	WILDLIFE
77°38′S, 166°24′E	Hut from Scott's *Terra Nova* expedition	Skua *190*
	Memorial cross to members of Imperial Trans-Antarctic Expedition	

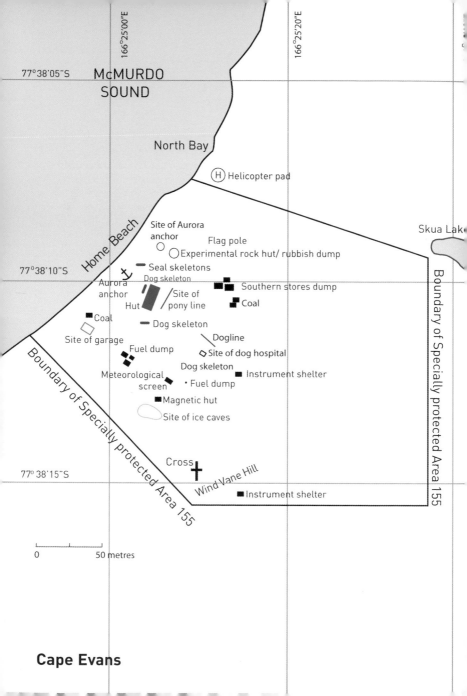

McMURDO SOUND

North Bay

Ⓗ Helicopter pad

Site of Aurora anchor

Flag pole

◯ Experimental rock hut/ rubbish dump

Home Beach

⚓ Seal skeletons

Dog skeleton

Aurora anchor

Hut

Site of pony line

Southern stores dump

Coal

Coal

Dog skeleton

Site of garage

Dogline

Fuel dump

◇ Site of dog hospital

Meteorological screen

Dog skeleton

Instrument shelter

Fuel dump

Magnetic hut

Site of ice caves

Cross

Wind Vane Hill

Instrument shelter

Skua Lake

Boundary of Specially protected Area 155

Boundary of Specially protected Area 155

77°38'05"S

77°38'10"S

77°38'15"S

166°25'00"E

166°25'20"E

0   50 metres

Cape Evans

→ artefacts outside the hut point to the rushed circumstances that befell this last expedition: the anchor on the shore is from the *Aurora*, which broke its moorings in May 1915 leaving a party of four men stranded ashore; the mummy is that of a sled dog, its collar still chained to a stake. On a hill behind the hut is a memorial cross to Aeneas Mackintosh, V.G. Hayward and Arnold Spencer-Smith, members of the expedition who died while laying supply depots further south. This site is also a protected Historic Monument (HSM17).

Since 1959, when the New Zealand government began restoration work, the hut has been repaired frequently and is maintained as a museum. The Antarctic Heritage Trust now cares for the building and the many artefacts in and around it. Be careful moving around inside – bulky parkas can inadvertently knock things off shelves in the tight confines of the poorly lit interior. Care should also be taken outside, where small artefacts are often hidden by the snow.

Cape Evans has been the site of two modern wintering expeditions, but their huts have been removed. In 1984 In the Footsteps of Scott established a base from which to re-enact Scott's trek to the pole, and in 1987 Greenpeace built a base here as well. Greenpeace later absorbed the Footsteps of Scott's hut, and then removed both structures at the end of their occupancy in 1992. The small green hut to the southwest is a refuge used by New Zealand parties when they work at Cape Evans.

places

The hut from Ernest Shackleton's first Antarctic expedition, the British Antarctic or *Nimrod*, is located on Cape Royds, the westernmost point of Ross Island. The site is named for Charles Royds, the meteorologist on Robert Scott's first Antarctic expedition. While the cape is home to 1754 pairs of nesting Adélie penguins, the hut, built in 1907, is the main attraction. It was from this modest prefabricated building that the first serious attempt was made to reach the geographic south pole. Shackleton, along with Frank Wild, Jameson Adams and Eric Marshall, struggled overland to within 182 kilometres (114 miles) of the pole in the summer of 1908–09.

The hut was later used by other expeditions, particularly the men from the 1914–17 Imperial Trans-Antarctic Expedition, who were marooned at Cape Evans without adequate supplies. The surplus left behind by Shackleton at Cape Royds saved their lives.

The hut is well preserved, but like the other historic buildings on Ross Island it was filled with snow and ice by the time the first restoration attempts were made in 1959. It is smaller than Scott's hut at Cape Evans, and as such has a particular charm. All visitors must abide by the strict rules set out in the site management plan, and must be accompanied by a certified guide. The area around the hut is designated an Antarctic Specially Protected Area (ASPA157), and a permit is required for entry. Only eight people are permitted inside the hut at one time, and care should be taken not to disturb any of the artefacts in and around the building. Be sure to knock all gravel from your boots before entering as the sharp volcanic scoria can cut the floor easily. →

places

GEOGRAPHIC LOCATION	POINTS OF INTEREST	WILDLIFE
77°33'S, 166°09'E	Hut from Shackleton's *Nimrod* expedition Adélie penguin rookery	Adélie penguin South polar skua *190*

→ The Adélie rookery here is the southernmost penguin breeding site in the world. The penguin population has fluctuated with varying ice conditions in recent years. In 1997 there were 3933 pairs, but by 2007 the population had dropped to 1754 pairs. Human disturbance had a big impact in the 1960s, when the colony was frequently visited by helicopters from McMurdo Station. These noisy visitors disturbed the nesting birds and the population fell by almost 50 percent before flight policies changed. The penguin colony and its seaward approaches are now designated an Antarctic Specially Protected Area (ASPA121). A permit is required to enter this area. The New Zealand government maintains a small green refuge hut east of the historic site. South polar skuas nest at Cape Royds, among the volcanic rock.

places

McMurdo Station

Scott Base

The largest human population in Antarctica resides on a small finger of volcanic rock pointing south into the Ross Ice Shelf. The United States operates McMurdo Station, which has a summer population of up to 1200, amid an atmosphere that more resembles a small American town than a scientific base. The station is equipped with housing, offices, laboratories, workshops and many of the cultural amenities you expect to find in a self-sufficient village, including several bars and a church. The sheer size of McMurdo means it also has some facilities unique in Antarctica, including an ATM machine, a bowling alley, aerobics classes and an intramural volleyball league.

Scientific research is the main reason for the presence of any base on the continent (but see Political Antarctica, page 21), and McMurdo is a productive facility with top-quality research churned out every year. The Albert Crary Laboratory is the pride of the station, and better equipped than many university facilities elsewhere in the world.

McMurdo Station is also the staging area and support base for a number of inland field camps, as well as for the substantial station that the United States operates at the geographic south pole. As with all Antarctic bases, the population plummets just before the winter sets in, and most years only 100 to 200 people remain during the coldest months. The National Science Foundation, which runs the United States Antarctic Program and the base, has been slow to appreciate the public relations value of accepting tourists on the station. However, attitudes have mollified and these days visitors will usually be given a guided tour of the science labs, dormitories and other buildings. →

places

GEOGRAPHIC LOCATION
77°51'S, 166°46'E

POINTS OF INTEREST
Largest settlement in Antarctica (McMurdo)
Two very productive scientific stations
Hut from Scott's *Discovery* expedition
Gift shops

→ A small wooden building stands near the shore at McMurdo, dwarfed by the modern construction all around. This is Discovery Hut, one of the oldest buildings in Antarctica. A prefabricated structure, it was erected by members of Robert Scott's *Discovery* expedition of 1901–04 for use as an onshore workplace; the men generally slept on board the *Discovery*, which in winter was only a short walk away over the sea ice. The hut was used by subsequent expeditions to the region, including Ernest Shackleton's *Nimrod* expedition of 1907–09, Scott's *Terra Nova* expedition of 1910–13, and finally by the Imperial Trans-Antarctic Expedition of 1914–17.

It remained snow-packed but well preserved until the Americans arrived to establish McMurdo Station in 1956. Shortly thereafter, New Zealand historians began excavating the ice that had built up inside, and today the hut is an Historic Monument under the Antarctic Treaty system (HSM18). It is maintained by the Antarctic Heritage Trust. All visitors must be accompanied by an appropriately certified guide. Nearby is a memorial cross to George Vince, a seaman on *Discovery* who in 1902 slipped down a snow slope while sledging in a blizzard, fell into the sea and died. His body was never recovered. This site is also a designated Historic Monument (HSM17).

Three kilometres (2 miles) away on the other side of a small hill lies Scott Base, a scientific station operated by New Zealand. The population at this cosy little station reaches up to 85 in summer, with about 15 people overwintering. A road connects it with McMurdo and the two stations share the logistics of moving cargo and people to and from Antarctica. However, each is set up to operate independently of the other.

Scott Base is compact and well designed, with most buildings connected by internal corridors. It has a completely different and more informal atmosphere than McMurdo, with staff from all positions mixing with little distinction between scientists and support personnel.

places

As Antarctic destinations go, there is none more spectacular than the Ross Ice Shelf. The vast ice cliffs of the northern edge extend for over 700 km (420 miles) and the surface, flat as a table, stretches southward for about 793 km (496 miles). Overall, the ice shelf covers about 520,000 sq km (200,000 sq miles), making it about the same size as Thailand, or twice the state of New York. Most visitors will see it from a ship sailing alongside the cliffs and from this perspective you can truly appreciate why its discoverer, James Ross, dubbed it the Ice Barrier in 1841. The cliffs form a fortress wall that in most places rises about 20m (65 feet) above sea level. The average thickness of the ice is about 370 m (1200 feet).

Ice shelves form where a large volume of glacial ice pours off land and coalesces in a protected bay. The merged glaciers then continue flowing forward over the surface of the sea and their flat surface reflects this smoothest of substrates underneath.

At its leading edge the Ross Ice Shelf is vulnerable to the warming ocean, and the forces of tides and currents. When these forces are strong enough, a piece of shelf breaks off and forms a tabular iceberg. The position of the edge of the shelf has remained relatively constant in the last century as the amount of ice breaking off is roughly equal to the amount feeding in from the south.

The largest iceberg ever known was spotted in the Ross Sea in 1955, and was about the same size as Belgium. Near the eastern end of the shelf is a persistent cleft known as the Bay of Whales. Roald Amundsen set up his winter base here for his journey to the geographic south pole in 1911. His hut has long since disappeared out to sea on a tabular iceberg.

places

GEOGRAPHIC LOCATION
81°30'S 175°00'W
(and vicinity)

POINTS OF INTEREST
Huge ice cliffs
World's largest piece
of floating ice

Many ships call into the Falkland Islands on their way to or from Antarctica. These stops usually turn out to be a pleasant surprise for those on board. Located 477 km (296 miles) east of southern Argentina, the Falklands are a rare mix of wildlife hotspot and delightful inhabited outpost. Comprising over 700 islands, the archipelago has a human population of around 4000, and a sea-bird population that dwarfs that. For wildlife lovers the Falklands are a fantastic destination. Unlike other subantarctic islands, they can be visited independently by scheduled flights.

GEOGRAPHY

The Falklands is an archipelago consisting of two main islands, East and West, with a prodigious scattering of smaller islands, of which only eleven are permanently inhabited. The group covers an area about the size of the state of Connecticut, or slightly more than Jamaica. It lies just downstream of the Drake Passage, a bottleneck in the massive Circumpolar Current that sweeps around the globe. The cold, nutrient-rich waters carried by this current flow north past the islands, making them a prime location for marine life, including sea birds and seals.

At first glance the Falklands seem stark and desolate. Their latitude of around 51°S has northern hemisphere equivalents in southern Laborador, London and Russia's Kamchatka Peninsula, but as small land masses surrounded by cold waters they have a much cooler climate than these more continental areas. They are constantly raked by strong winds from the Southern Ocean and have no naturally occurring trees, so their exposure to the weather can seem daunting at times. In summer, however, temperatures are comparatively mild, around 9°C/ 48°F, and the sun shines more often than not.

Since the Falklands are close enough to South America to be in the 'rain shadow' of the Andes, they are not particularly wet: average annual precipitation ranges from 399–646 mm (15–25 in), most of it falling as rain. They are hilly in places, particularly in the north of the two main islands, and these upland areas do get snow each winter. However, as this melts away during the summer there are no glaciers. The highest point is Mount Usborne, which reaches 705 m/2312 ft.

GEOLOGY

The Falklands have never been physically attached to South America. One of the most wayward fragments of the ancient supercontinent Gondwana, they began as a sliver attached to the eastern side of what is now South Africa 400 million years ago. As the tectonic plates shifted, the scrap of continental crust holding the Falklands made its way across the widening Atlantic until it reached its current position some 150 million years ago. The islands have been glaciated several times, most recently in the Pleistocene epoch that ended about 10,000 years ago. The rocks are mostly sedimentary varieties such as quartzite and sandstone, although there are some intrusions of igneous basalt and dolerite.

d from Stanley to Mount Pleasant military base

y Cove, close to Stanley

places

WILDLIFE

In addition to the rich ocean, another factor determining the flora and fauna of the Falklands is the islands' proximity to South America. Most plants and animals here are also found on the mainland. It is likely that seeds and birds in particular became established after being blown eastward from Patagonia. The process continues, and each year many South American land birds turn up in the Falklands.

The most obvious wildlife are the sea birds. Literally millions of petrels, albatrosses, penguins, gulls and cormorants inhabit the Falklands. These birds all feed at sea but need solid land on which to nest. As the Falklands are the only option in this corner of the ocean, the birds pack into colonies with thousands of nests. Black-browed albatrosses can be viewed on several western islands such as New, West Point, Saunders and Steeple Jason. Rockhopper penguins nest between the peaty pedestals of albatross nests and on steep rocky slopes. Their numbers have decreased dramatically in the past 70 years, possibly as a result of reduction in food availability caused by warming sea temperatures.

If you are on a ship in near-shore waters, you will see southern giant petrels (page 174), white-chinned petrels (page 176), and a number of prion species, including the Antarctic prion (page 184). Magellanic and blue-eyed cormorants frequent rocky ledges along some coasts, and ocean-going waterfowl abound. In Stanley's harbour, kelp geese, upland geese, crested ducks and flightless steamer ducks are the most obvious species.

Marine mammals are also plentiful along the coasts. Commerson's and Peale's dolphins often play in the pressure wave at the bow of moving ships, and will sometimes stay right into the shallows. Killer whales regularly visit the shores of Sea Lion Island, but are not often seen elsewhere.

Sea Lion Island is the site of one of the few breeding populations of southern elephant seals in the Falklands. These enormous blubber slugs were formerly much more common, but unrestricted sealing in the eighteenth and nineteenth centuries depleted stocks severely. South American fur seals and sea lions were also targets, but their populations have recovered well. Fur seals, which prefer rocky shorelines, are concentrated on the western islands, while the larger sea lions make their homes on sandy beaches.

Sea lion

places

Black-crowned night heron

Striated caracara

Sea lion harem, with one large male

Commerson's dolphins

HUMAN HISTORY

Errant sailors from European countries were the first confirmed human visitors to the Falklands, but there is some evidence that Yahgan Indians from Tierra del Fuego may have reached the islands earlier. Given that the Yahgans used canoes and travelled extensively around the Fuegian coast, it would not be surprising if a few unfortunate families had been blown downwind and ended up on the Falklands. A small number of hunting tools and pieces of canoes have been found, but the strongest evidence is perhaps the presence of the warrah or Falklands Islands fox, also known as the Antarctic wolf, an animal that closely resembles the small hunting dogs used by the Yahgan. Its presence in the islands is difficult to explain without human assistance. (Very tame, warrahs were hunted to extinction by European settlers in 1876.) However, there is no evidence that these early Yahgan castaways settled here.

In the 1500s and 1600s, a few European ships were also blown downwind from South America and landed in the Falklands. Unlike the Yahgans, these sailors were successful at repairing their vessels and returned home to tell of the new land they had found. The names of the first Europeans to see the islands are not known, but they were presumably Portuguese as the islands appeared on two early maps from that country drawn in 1519 and 1586. Records show that a Spanish ship was in the islands for a few winter months in 1540, and in 1592 Englishman John Davis sighted the islands. Unlike the Spanish before him, who carried maps showing the islands, Davis thought he had discovered new land.

Settlement was a long time coming: it was not until 1764 that a permanent colony was established. This pioneering effort was the work of France's Louis-Antoine de Bouganville, who established Port Louis at a bay in the north-east of East Falkland. Most of the settlers sailed from Saint Malo, and the islands were sometimes called the Malouines. In Argentina, they continue to be known as Islas Malvinas, the Spanish version of this name.

In 1765 a British contingent under John Byron spent two weeks on Saunders Island in the west of the Falklands, and after another year the British returned and established their first settlement, unaware there was a thriving French colony on East Falkland. Once each colony became aware

places

of the other, the Falklands became the object of international bickering, diplomatic negotiation and hostile combat that continues to this day.

The fate of the Falklands has fluctuated with the relative strength of each possessor. The Spanish took over Port Louis from their ally France in 1767, based on the claim to land in the new world given them under the Treaty of Utrecht. Shortly afterwards the Spanish and British began several decades of expulsions and posturing. The last of these came in 1833, when Britain forced out the Argentinian colonists – Argentina having taken over as Spain's influence in South America waned. The Falklands then remained under British control until 1982, when Argentina invaded and occupied the islands for 74 days before British troops wrested them back. The war cost 910 lives, including three Falklanders. Argentina still maintains its claim, although this is not recognised by many countries outside of Latin America. Britain's interest in its costly colony had declined in the 1960s and '70s, but in the aftermath of the war the government poured in money, improving infrastructure and modernising the lives of the islanders.

GOVERNMENT

Officially, the Falkland Islands are an Overseas Territory of the United Kingdom, with a governor appointed by the British monarch. However, they are largely self-governed by a council of locally elected representatives, who handle all portfolios except foreign affairs and defence. For a century and a half the islands were fully dependent on economic subsidies, at great expense to the British taxpayer. With the establishment of an exclusive fishery zone in 1986 and the sale of licences to foreign vessels, they became financially self-sufficient in all but defence. They have their own postage stamps and currency, the Falkland Island pound, which is equal in value to the pound sterling.

The last census, in 2006, counted a population of 2478 with just over half born here. Stanley, the capital, is home to 85 percent. When the military and support personnel stationed at the Mount Pleasant garrison are included, the total population is closer to 4000.

places

South Georgia, an island in the South Atlantic Ocean about 900 miles south-east of the Falkland Islands, is one of the world's most remarkable wildlife locations. Although it lies at 54°S, about the same latitude as Cape Horn, it is much colder than South America because it is surrounded by chilly Antarctic waters. However, despite being south of the Antarctic Convergence, the sea around it does not freeze. Wildlife resides here year-round: there is no winter exodus as in Antarctica. The diversity is also much greater: over 30 species of birds breed in South Georgia, compared to only 15 in Antarctica.

The island is shaped liked a croissant that has been partially straightened, and has a spine of tall, heavily glaciated mountains up to 2934 metres/9535 feet. There are no trees but many other plants thrive; the tallest are a type of tussock grass. The south and west coasts face into the prevailing winds and are routinely battered by storms from the Southern Ocean. The rugged headlands and small bays host substantial numbers of breeding seals and penguins, but it is on the milder north side of the island that the wildlife populations really explode. This relatively sheltered coast is indented by many deep bays, and most beaches are crowded with brightly coloured king penguins, fast-moving fur seals, and lumpy elephant seals. The sloping terrain above supports nesting albatrosses and various petrels.

South Georgia

WILDLIFE

South Georgia is home to about 450,000 pairs of flamboyant king penguins and 1.1 million pairs of macaroni penguins, as well as thousands of gentoos and chinstraps. Four species of albatross also breed here, as do 13 species of petrel. The beaches are crowded with southern elephant seals and Antarctic fur seals; in some places landing is not physically possible because the fur seals are so thickly packed. A small population of Weddell seals breeds in Drygalski Fiord at the southern end of the island. There are no native land mammals, but in 1911 Norwegien whalers introduced reindeer as a source of meat and for sport, and several herds still roam the island. Rats and mice have also established themselves after jumping ship during the sealing and whaling periods.

Birdwatchers will be particularly keen to see the two endemic species found here: the South Georgia pintail and the South Georgia pipit. The pipit, the only songbird on the island, has a much reduced range due to predation by rats. It is now confined to isolated pockets on the main island, and to small offshore islets still free of these introduced rodents.

Reindeer

Mount Paget and Allardyce Range

GEOLOGY

South Georgia is composed of mainly sedimentary rocks that have much in common with those found in the southern Andes of Chile and Argentina. The island is part of the Scotia Arc, a ridge of continental crust that runs in a wide, easterly looping parabola from Tierra del Fuego to the Antarctic Peninsula. Thirty-five million years ago South Georgia was attached to South America, but over time it has separated and been pushed eastwards by the movements of tectonic plates.

HISTORY

While today South Georgia appears wild and untamed, it was once well populated and highly industrialised. A French merchant from London, Antoine de la Roché, may have seen the island as early as 1675, but it was certainly sighted by a Spanish ship, *Léon*, in 1756 and named Isla San Pedro for the saint whose feast day coincided with their visit. (It is also noted on maps as St Peter's Island and Île de St Pierre.) James Cook visited in 1775, and ignoring its existing name decided to name it after his sovereign, George III. Cook was not particularly impressed with the island, but he did note the abundance of seals. This almost casual observation in his published report was enough to start the first wave of human activity on the island. Commercial sealers harvested Antarctic fur seals in the late 1700s and early 1800s, and hunted the

places

species almost to extinction. Hundreds of thousands of fur-seal pelts were taken from the island, and hunting finally halted only when there were not enough seals left to make the trip to the far south economically viable. Elephant seals were also harvested and depleted for the oil within their thick blubber.

The whaling era was the next chapter of marine mammal plunder. The industry was set up initially in 1904 by Norway's Captain Carl Larsen at Grytviken: the name means 'little pot', a reference to the rusted iron pots from former sealing camps. Larsen, who was also a noted Antarctic explorer and scientist, established a joint venture with Argentinians in a company called Compañia Argentina de Pesca. Whaling became widespread. Commercial whalers set up shore stations to process the dead whales brought in by their fleets of catcher boats. In the 1920s factory ships were added to the arsenal. The industry became so efficient that even the fastest whales didn't stand a chance.

By 1964, when the last shore stations closed, hundreds of thousands of whales had been taken from South Georgian waters. In the 1937–38 season alone, deep-sea whaling killed over 46,000, almost 90 percent of the world's catch for that year. At the peak of whaling, South Georgia had over 2000 inhabitants, most of them Norwegian. The rusting iron buildings of their stations are prominent in many sheltered coves.

As the last civilised place before Antarctica, South Georgia was also visited by members of many scientific and adventure expeditions. The most notable was Ernest Shackleton, who died here in 1922 during his *Quest* expedition and is buried in the Whaler's Cemetery at Grytviken. Shackleton had visited the island earlier, at the end of his disastrous Imperial Trans-Antarctic Expedition in 1916. After the expedition's ship *Endurance* was crushed by ice and sank far to the south, the men made a treacherous journey over the sea ice to finally reach land on uninhabited Elephant Island in Antarctica. With the winter upon them, six then set sail to South Georgia in a small boat (6 m/20 ft) to seek help. The journey across the stormy Southern Ocean took them 15 days, and thanks largely to the navigational skills of Captain Frank Worsley they found the island. However, they landed on the uninhabited south-west coast: all the whaling stations were on the north-east.

places

LEFT *Grave of Ernest Shackleton, Whaler's Cemetery, Grytviken*
OPPOSITE *Whaling debris, Grytviken*

Stromness Bay and whaling station

The icy, mountainous interior of the island was unknown and unmapped, but without any proper climbing equipment three of the men hiked across the island and arrived safely at Stromness whaling station, where they organised a rescue mission for the men on Elephant Island. A popular excursion sees many visitors hike over the last leg of this journey, from Fortuna Bay to Stromness. The route is unglaciated and the trip can be made by those in reasonable fitness. Grytviken also featured in the 1982 Falklands war as the site of the first battle to reassert British sovereignty in the region.

GOVERNMENT

South Georgia is an Overseas Territory of the United Kingdom and administered by a government largely based in Stanley, Falkland Islands. The governor of the Falklands is also the commissioner of the government of South Georgia and South Sandwich Islands. Argentina claims the island as part of its claim to the Malvinas/Falklands, but this is not widely recognised.

There are no true permanent residents, but a dozen or so officials (depending on the time of year) are installed at the administrative centre at King Edward Point, near Grytviken. They all work on fixed-term contracts for government or research positions. Fishing is by far the leading industry and the government sells licences (and fresh water) to vessels wanting to fish within 200 miles of the island. A landing fee charged to visitors makes tourism the next largest earner, with philately a distant third. South Georgia and the South Sandwich Islands have their own postage stamps and these are popular with visitors.

Norwegian church, Grytviken

POINTS OF INTEREST

Local regulations dictate that all visitors must stop at Grytviken for immigration formalities, but this former whaling station also has much to enjoy. The rusting metal provides a vivid reminder of the island's industrial past, while a small museum in the former manager's house displays many aspects of the island's natural and human history. It also has an extensive gift shop. The grave of Ernest Shackleton can be found in a prominent position in the Whaler's Cemetery. Please be careful not to disturb any of the graves while visiting, and keep the gate closed to keep out the seals. Grytviken is not home to any large breeding colonies, but the shoreline is often visited by young fur and elephant seals and the occasional penguin. Walking onshore is relatively easy, and the terrain in Grytviken itself is quite even.

Antarctic fur seals are prevalent along practically all shorelines and their raucous, busy life is often best viewed from a small boat just offshore. If the density of seals is sparse enough to allow a landing, take particular care not to disturb the animals, and be wary of the large males: they will defend their territory with great vigour and violence. Southern elephant seals also crowd the beaches and in the summer months are usually piled up in mobs of moulting individuals.

Large colonies of king penguins are found in many bays, but the most popular sites for viewing them are Salisbury Plain, St Andrews Bay, Royal Bay and Gold Harbour. These birds are quite tolerant of visitors, but visitors should take extra care not to disturb nesting individuals, distinguishable by their 'pot bellies' and uniform spacing.

Grey-headed and black-browed albatrosses nest in dense colonies along some of the steeper slopes and well above the tide line. Visits to these areas requires climbing up steep grassy slopes. Be cautious and always stay well outside the edge of the colony. Light-mantled sooty albatrosses nest on these same grassy slopes, but they do not form colonies. On Prion Island, visitors have the opportunity to see wandering albatrosses on their nests. These largest of South Georgia's birds nest on pedestals of mud widely dispersed among tussock grass on the island's summit.

WEATHER AND CLOTHING

South Georgia is generally warmer than Antarctica, but it can be chilly and windy. Most people find they are comfortable in the same clothes they would wear in Antarctica. The parkas issued by most tour operators can be happily used here. Air temperatures in the summer months usually range from 5–10°C (42–55°F), and wind and rain are possible. As always, it is best to wear layers of clothing.

places

TOP *Gold Harbour*
LEFT *Southern giant petrel chick* RIGHT *Antarctic fur seals*

Gentoo penguin and Weddell seal

Life in Antarctica

Chinstrap colony, Baily Head, Deception Island. The hills are covered in algae (Prasiola crispa), with a little moss.

The Antarctic ecosystem is unique: most of the organisms here are found nowhere else. There are fish with body temperatures of –1.9°C, sea-lice that grow to the size of your hand, seals whose teeth are modified as strainers. While the number of species on and around Antarctica is not vast compared with that of other major ecosystems (for example, rain forest, grasslands or tropical reefs), the abundance of animal life is staggering. Krill, a small marine crustacean, number in the million billions. The continent also supports huge colonies of penguins, and is home to the most abundant marine mammal in the world, the crabeater seal.

Because of the low species diversity, Antarctic food chains are relatively simple. Some have only a few steps between the base level (plants) and the top-level predators (whales). This simplicity makes Antarctica an excellent place to learn about the relationships between plants and animals, but the same trait also makes for great vulnerability. There are few options for survival in this delicately balanced ecosystem if one or more key species is wiped out. The over-exploitation of marine resources, the ozone hole, and rising temperatures brought on by global climate change are all threats that could seriously damage the fragile south.

Temperature and life

Temperature governs the distribution of all life on Earth. Temperatures below the freezing point of water are lethal to all but a few organisms. Ice is the enemy, bursting cells and dehydrating tissues. For this reason the interior of Antarctica, where temperatures drop to below –80°C, is effectively lifeless. The vast snow- and ice-covered areas are devoid of plants and animals, apart from occasional humans.

However, around the fringes of the continent, on the outer islands and in the surrounding waters there is a rich variety of wildlife and, perhaps surprisingly, one of the more productive ecosystems on the planet. Living in the coldest place on Earth, Antarctic plants and animals have evolved highly specialised adaptations to cope with the dangerously low temperatures. And this is also one of the most spectacular regions for observing wildlife. Whales, seals and penguins all abound against a backdrop of stunning beauty.

THE TERRESTRIAL ECOSYSTEM

Less than 0.4 percent of the Antarctic continent and surrounding islands is permanently or seasonally free of ice. There is thus a paucity of life on Antarctica's actual land mass, especially when compared to terrestrial ecosystems elsewhere on Earth. The main factor limiting the distribution of land plants and animals is not the cold but the lack of available water. However, in the few snow-free areas dotted around the continent there is some respite from the bitter conditions during summer, when the heat from the sun is enough to raise temperatures above freezing. Water, the elixir of life, becomes available and plants and animals are able to survive.

Even so, the land-based flora and fauna of Antarctica are meagre in number and lacking in diversity. The large number of penguins, sea birds and seals seen on land are only visitors, coming ashore to reproduce or rest. Part of the marine ecosystem, they spend most of their lives feeding or being fed upon at sea.

Land-based life
- two species of flowering plants
- more than 260 species of lichen
- red, green, yellow & brown snow algae
- more than 70 species of mosses
- flightless midges
- mites
- springtails
- nematodes (round worms)
- no land-based mammals or birds

life in Antarctica

Plants

With almost the entire continent covered by ice and snow, there is a lack of suitable habitat for plants to grow. Total darkness during winter, a lack of liquid water and virtually no soil all conspire against luxuriant plant growth. Only in the coastal regions of Antarctica is there enough bare land and soil for plants to put down their roots, and for water to become available during the 'warmer' months.

Red lichen, Half Moon Island

The most impressive diversity of plants occurs on the west coast of the Antarctic Peninsula and on the South Shetland Islands. This is perhaps not surprising, given that these locations are at lower latitudes with relatively warmer temperatures and are free of ice and snow, especially during the summer months. These coastal ice-free areas also support large penguin rookeries during summer and it is here that ornithogenic ('bird-created') soils develop. Penguin droppings, feathers and bird carcasses break down to produce soil that is rich in nitrogen and phosphate.

The few plants in Antarctica are simple. There are no trees, bushes or other plants that grow more than a few centimetres in height. Lichens, mosses and algae dominate, although there are also two flowering plants: a grass and a pearlwort. Despite 24 hours of daylight during summer, the growth rate of plants in Antarctica is extremely slow. Some grow no more than 0.5 mm (0.02 in) per year, so great care needs to be taken to avoid treading on them.

Algae require water, nutrients and light to grow. In summer, when temperatures rise above freezing point, red, green and yellow algae take advantage of water from snow-melt to grow and reproduce. During mid to late summer, blooms of unicellular snow algae can be seen in patches of melting snow. These patches can span several hundred metres. Red is the most widespread colour, but the organism exhibiting this is in fact classified as a green algae.

Yellow lichen

Moss

Hair grass

Pearlwort

Lichens adorn the rocky outcrops in a captivating array of colours; their bright yellow, orange, green and black hues provide a striking contrast to the predominant blue, white and grey of the Antarctic landscape. There are more than 260 species and the greatest diversity is found on the South Shetland Islands.

Lichens are symbiotic organisms in which algae and fungi cohabit. They have no roots, and instead acquire water vapour from the air and absorb it across their outer surface. They are one of only a few organisms capable of surviving conditions below −20°C. They grow incredibly slowly – only 0.4 mm (0.016 in) a year – and some large individuals of the species, *Rhizocarpon geographicum*, have been found to be more than 4000 years old.

There are more than 70 species of moss (*bryophytes*) in Antarctica. These primitive plants grow in small clumps between crevices in rock but can also be seen covering vast areas, such as on the slopes in the extinct volcanic crater of Deception Island.

The hair grass (*Deschampsia antarctica*) and the pearlwort (*Colobanthus quitensis*) are the only flowering plants that occur in Antarctica. Found mainly around penguin colonies, where they can take advantage of ornithogenic soils, they generally occur in small clumps.

life in Antarctica

Land-based animals

In Antarctica there are no large terrestrial herbivorous mammals as in Arctic regions: there is simply not enough for them to eat. Freezing and desiccation are also potentially lethal forces.

Land-based fauna are dominated by invertebrates, which include nematode worms, tardigrades (microscopic animals, also known as water bears), rotifers (tiny, aquatic, filter-feeding animals that live in damp moss and under stones), and a few insects and mites. Most of these animals grow no bigger than 2 mm (0.08 in) in body length, and are found under rocks and within moss beds, where they gain some protection from the harsh conditions. The organically rich soils around penguin colonies often support large numbers of nematode worms – up to several million per square metre.

Springtails

There are about 20 species of free-living (as opposed to parasitic) insects in continental and maritime Antarctica. However, springtails (*Collembola – Cryptopygus antarcticus*) are the only ones found on the mainland. Springtails are small, primitive, wingless insects that feed on algae and moss and can be found living under rocks and in crevices. Mites can also be found cohabiting with springtails. Some species prey on the springtails, while others are herbivorous.

Ice formation in tissues will kill most animals. To survive, many Antarctica invertebrates fill themselves with cryoprotectants – 'anti-freeze' compounds such as glycerol and sugars – which allow them to remain super-cooled. In this state, their body water remains in liquid form, despite their body temperature being below freezing point. Nonetheless, these animals are living on the edge, as they run the risk of spontaneously freezing and becoming inanimate miniature ice-cubes.

Killeer whales, Paradise Harbour

THE MARINE ECOSYSTEM

At the core of biodiversity and productivity in Antarctica is the marine ecosystem, and many of the plants and animals living in these waters are both unique and astonishing. In stark contrast to the impoverished land mass of Antarctica, the Southern Ocean and seas that encircle the continent support rich and abundant life. Moreover, these marine plants and animals experience stable and fairly benign conditions. There is plenty of available water, and sea temperatures can go no lower than a relatively warm –1.9°C (28.9°F), after which sea water freezes.

The near-constant water temperatures are, however, punctuated by strong seasonal changes, with the higher latitudes experiencing 24 hours of darkness a day in winter and 24 hours of sunlight a day in summer. The cold Antarctic waters are rich in dissolved minerals and oxygen. When the sun shines for 24 hours a day, the conditions provide a potent cocktail for life to flourish, grow and reproduce.

The Southern Ocean

The Southern Ocean (formerly known as the Antarctic Ocean) encircles Antarctica and connects the Pacific, Atlantic and Indian Oceans. The ocean's northern boundary is defined by the Antarctic Convergence (Polar Front), located at 50–60°S. At the Convergence, the northerly flowing surface waters of the Antarctic sink below the warmer subantarctic surface waters and there is a rapid drop in surface temperature of 3–4°C (5.5–7°F). This large temperature change not only means the region is often shrouded in mist and fog, but also provides an effective barrier for many marine organisms, with the southerly Antarctic waters being too cold for most.

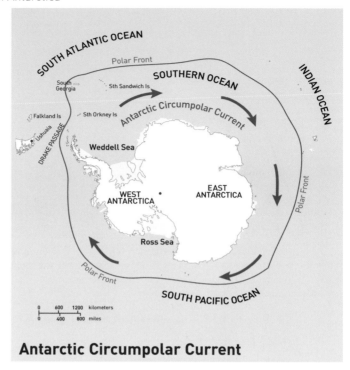

Antarctic Circumpolar Current

Two main currents move sea water around Antarctica. Close to the continent, surface waters flow from east to west (counter-clockwise circulation). This is the Antarctic Coastal Current, driven by the prevailing easterly winds. Further northwards, from 45–60°S, is the Antarctic Circumpolar Current, which flows west to east and is the major current in the Southern Ocean. This current allows the exchange of water between the major oceans of the world; it acts like a huge oceanic conveyer belt, transporting not only nutrients but also heat, which has a significant role in controlling the Earth's climate.

The narrowest gap through which this current must flow is the Drake Passage, between the bottom tip of South America and the northern tip of the Antarctic Peninsula. Here the current moves more than 130 million cubic m (170 million cubic yards) of water per second – 8000 times the flow rate of the Mississippi River. On a smaller scale, in embayments along the coastline of Antarctica the currents are localised and form clockwise gyres, or circular currents, that help to concentrate nutrients. The Ross and Weddell Seas are two such embayments.

Another important feature of the Southern Ocean is the annual fluctuation in sea ice. After winter, the coverage of sea ice is at its peak, covering some 19–20 million sq km (11.8–12.5 million sq miles) of the Southern Ocean, and in the process doubling the size of Antarctica.

The frozen sea water, 1–3 m (3–9 ft) thick, provides an important habitat for plants and animals, both above and below the surface. Seals and penguins use the sea ice (and icebergs) as a place to haul out and rest. Crabeater, Ross and leopard seals use it as a convenient birthing spot. The underside of sea ice is important in providing a habitat for algae growth, a nursery for krill and a refuge for icefish. Large open areas of water among the sea ice (technically known as polynyas) also provide access points for penguins and seals to reach the sea during early spring.

Crabeater seals on sea ice

Southern giant petrel after feasting on a freshly dead southern elephant seal pup.

The marine food web

Microbes, plants and animals form complex associations and interactions with each other. Collectively, this is known as a food web. With herbivores feeding on plants, and carnivores on herbivores, food webs can have many levels. Typically, there are five or more steps from the plants at the base to the predators at the top. Unusually, the Antarctic marine ecosystem is characterised by shortcuts where several levels are bypassed.

Driving the Antarctic ecosystem are phytoplankton – microscopic algae. Feeding on these floating plants are herbivores, among which krill is the keystone species. Krill provides a source of food for many predators, including those at the *top* of the food web – the penguins, sea birds, seals and whales – thereby cutting out other levels of the web. Although the phytoplankton–krill–whale thread is the most common, it forms only part of a complex web of life in which other herbivores and carnivores, such as fish and squid, play an important role.

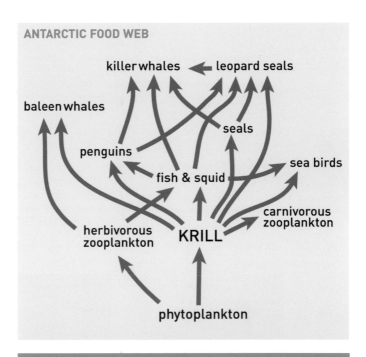

ANTARCTIC FOOD WEB

killer whales ◄ leopard seals

baleen whales

seals

penguins

fish & squid

sea birds

carnivorous zooplankton

herbivorous zooplankton

KRILL

phytoplankton

Typical food web
I   Primary production – phytoplankton (mainly diatoms)
II   small zooplankton – for example, copepods
       (a crustacean)
III   large zooplankton – for example, krill
IV   fish
V   large fish, penguins, seals
VI   whales, killer whales, leopard seals

Antarctic shortcuts
krill (III feed on I)
baleen whales (VI feed on III)

Plankton

Plankton, for the most part, are small organisms that literally float in the oceans and are at the whim of currents and tides.

Phytoplankton are floating plants, and a crucial part of almost all aquatic food webs. In the Southern Ocean, they are the key primary producers of the ecosystem, converting energy from sunlight through the process of photosynthesis. The phytoplankton take advantage of the long hours of daylight during summer, and water rich in nutrients and carbon dioxide, to grow and bloom. In Antarctic waters, phytoplankton are predominantly diatoms – single-celled algae with elaborate skeletons made from silica. Dinoflagellates, another type of phytoplankton, also exist here but are less common.

Zooplankton are drifting animals that feed on other plankton. They vary in size from microscopic, single-celled animals to small crustaceans and fish larvae, to large jellyfish with tentacles many metres long.

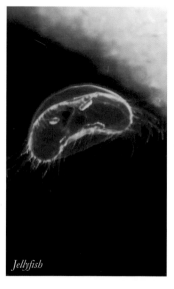

Jellyfish

Krill

The best known zooplankton are krill (*euphausiids*), small, shrimp-like crustaceans that occur in large swarms in the Southern Ocean. Densities of greater than 20,000 individuals per cubic metre have been reported over many square kilometres and extending down to depths of 40–50 m (130–165 ft). The biomass of krill in the Antarctic makes up tens of millions of tonnes, with a significant amount consumed by fish, penguins, seals and whales.

Eleven species of krill are found in Antarctic waters. The most common is *Euphausia superba*. Measuring about 6 cm (2.3 in) long, *Euphausia superba* can produce 2000 to 3000 eggs a year and live for six or seven years.

Krill are filter-feeders; they use fine combs on their forelimbs to sieve small phytoplankton from the water. During winter they congregate beneath the sea ice, where they feed on algae and retreat from predators. The sea ice also acts as a nursery ground for their larvae. The abundance of krill appears to be related to the area of sea ice that forms over winter: the greater the area of sea ice, the greater the number of krill.

life in Antarctica

Sea-floor-dwelling organisms

In shallow water and intertidal zones, where the sea can freeze solid from top to bottom, life is sparse owing to the freezing conditions and ice-scouring; limpets and periwinkles are some of the few animals found here. But in deeper water and on the sea floor there is a rich variety of anemones, soft corals, worms, crustaceans, starfish, sea urchins and fish. Some of these animals grow much bigger than similar species in temperate or tropical waters. Starfish can measure 1 m (3.2 ft) in diameter, worms grow longer than 2 m (6.5 ft), sea spiders (not true spiders) are bigger than a dinner plate and sea-lice are hand-size. The ability to grow unusually large is attributable to the cold conditions and high levels of dissolved oxygen in the water.

Limpets

Sea-floor dwelling fish Trematomus bernachii

Fish

Of the 30,000 different species of fish worldwide, only about 120 are from waters around Antarctica. There are no sharks, and more than 60 percent of the fish belong to a single group, the *Nototbenioidei*. These fish are cold-water specialists and have evolved remarkable strategies to prevent freezing. In response to living in waters of −1.9°C (28.5°F), most Antarctic fish synthesise anti-freeze molecules, special protein-carbohydrate compounds that prevent ice from forming in the blood and tissues.

Icefish (*Channichthyids*) are unique among the vertebrates in that they have no red blood cells and carry oxygen dissolved in plasma. A blood sample from these fish is completely colourless. The lack of red blood cells is possible only in the cold Antarctic waters because of the high oxygen levels, and probably evolved as a means of reducing the blood's viscosity.

Many of the fish in Antarctica occur near the sea floor and in deep water, including the giant Antarctic toothfish and the larval-looking eelpout, a small bottom-dwelling fish that looks a bit like an eel.

Other vertebrates

At the top of the Antarctic food web are the large vertebrates: birds, seals and whales. All are carnivores and predators, feeding on the rich supply of food within the Southern Ocean. Krill is the chief food source for the leopard seals and crabeater seals, the baleen whales and many of the birds. Fish and squid are also important prey for birds, seals and whales, especially those species that are accomplished divers.

life in Antarctica

Light-mantled sooty albatross

Birds

Cape petrel

Sea birds

The very name 'sea bird' shows our human bias as land animals. We don't talk about 'land birds' because, as creatures of the land ourselves, we think any bird that lives there is normal and doesn't require a special appellation. But a bird that lives at sea really is something special. These birds amaze us because they live and thrive in the open ocean – an environment that is extremely hostile to us humans.

Although more than 70 percent of the planet is covered in water, only 3 percent of the world's 10,000 bird species are regarded as citizens of the sea. These birds are a variety of different types, united not by their ancestry but by their way of life. They all find food in the ocean, and most cover its vast expanses as if they were no obstacle. They cannot nest on the ocean, however, so they tend to congregate on the shores of islands and along coasts, often in large colonies.

All sea birds have a problem getting fresh water to drink, especially when in the middle of an ocean. To solve this, they drink sea water and eliminate the excess salt via glands located above their eyes. The very salty liquid produced by these glands drains from their nostrils and drips from the end of their bills. You will often observe sea birds with a runny nose: this is the salt gland at work.

Antarctic sea birds
- albatrosses & petrels
- penguins
- cormorants/shags
- gulls & skuas
- terns
- sheathbills

birds

Black-browed albatross

BODY FORM

The *Procellariiformes*, or 'tube-noses', include the albatrosses, shearwaters and petrels. These birds range far from land into the most remote corners of the oceans. They vary in size from the royal albatross (11 kg/24 lb) to the tiny storm petrels (45 g/1.6 oz). All species in the group have nostrils in prominent tubes on top of their beaks. They are unusual among birds in having an excellent sense of smell, which they use to find food in the vast stretches of seemingly empty ocean. Most tube-noses are excellent gliders, having long, narrow wings that are perfect for harnessing the winds near the sea surface. By tacking and changing the angle of their wings to the wind, they can cover hundreds of kilometres with hardly a wing-beat.

Penguins (*Sphenisciformes*) are closely related to the tube-noses. They are specialised for diving, and their short, stout stature on land makes for a torpedo-shaped body in the water. (For a more detailed look at the penguins, see pages 196–221.)

Cormorants are related to pelicans. If you look closely at a cormorant's throat, you will find a small membranous sac like a miniature pelican pouch. There is only one species of cormorant, or shag (the terms are synonymous) in Antarctica. This Antarctic cormorant, like others of the family, is a heavy bird and ponderous flier that needs to continuously flap its wings in order to stay in the air; you will seldom see a cormorant glide. They pursue their fishy prey underwater, swimming with their wings tucked in and paddling with their large webbed feet. Their long neck is useful for extending and grabbing fish. They are seldom seen far from land.

Gulls, skuas and terns are also usually seen only near the shore. They have a familiar body shape, with an upright stance and relatively large head. As fliers, gulls and skuas are good generalists: strong flappers but also adept at gliding. Terns are also excellent in the air, so much so that they seldom walk anywhere. Their legs are not very strong.

BEHAVIOUR

Except for the largest albatrosses, Antarctic sea birds breed every year. Nesting takes place in the short summer and involves a shared parental effort: both male and female take turns incubating eggs, feeding chicks and defending the nesting territory. Most species nest in colonies. This is a bonus for visitors, because it means if you find one bird you'll find many others close by.

Tube-noses feed in the open sea, where they take squid, krill, small crustaceans, and even offal and carrion. Many species are conspicuous because of their habit of following ships, and if you spend time on the stern of your vessel you are likely to get some wonderful views of albatrosses and petrels.

Birds follow ships because the vessel's movement often makes food available to them: the propellers churn up the water and bring otherwise inaccessible animals to the surface from many metres below. The wake of a ship is therefore a temporary buffet table that is under constant inspection by hungry birds. You may not see many of them alight and feed, but they will occasionally do so. That's all it takes to make following a ship worthwhile.

Black-browed albatross

Another common interaction between ships and tube-noses occurs because of the birds' propensity for landing on deck during the night. Many petrels are active at night-time and are attracted to the ship's lights. Disoriented when they get in close, they often crash-land on board and are unable to take off again because of the railings and scuppers. If they are still around at daybreak, they tend to seek a dark corner in which to hide. If you find a bird on the deck, leave it alone and notify a member of the ship's expedition team or crew. The birds are usually in fine health; they're just unable to take off on their own since they need a long runway to get airborne and ships' decks have too many obstacles. A boost over the rails is usually all they need to return to their normal place, gliding over the waves.

Shags do all their feeding underwater. After a dive, they pop to the surface and then laboriously take flight with a long run across the waves. Shags also dive to collect marine algae for their nests, and the sight of a fast-flapping shag zooming past with a beak full of seaweed is not uncommon during the summer. Unlike shags in many other continents, Antarctic cormorants do not hang their wings open to dry.

birds

IDENTIFICATION

The basic types of sea birds can be identified by their shapes, their behaviour and where they are encountered. Most petrels have long thin wings and are usually the only type of bird seen in the open ocean. Albatrosses are like a very large petrel, and some have wingspans of up to 3.5 m (11 ft).

Closer to the coast, shags (cormorants), gulls and terns may all be present, and to distinguish one from another you'll need to look carefully at the shape and size of the bird, and how it flaps. If it beats its wings furiously with no gliding, and looks as if it is only just keeping itself in the air, it is probably a shag. Gulls and skuas also flap their wings strongly, but they get more lift from each beat and also show a greater manoeuvrability.

Terns are the 'lightest' of Antarctic fliers in that each wing-beat seems to lift the bird higher in the air. They are also the only bird here with a forked tail.

Royal albatross

birds

SCIENTIFIC NAME
Thalassarche melanophris

POPULATION SIZE
700,000+ breeding pairs

DISTRIBUTION
breeds in subantarctic, mostly south Atlantic Ocean (Falkland Islands), but also Indian Ocean and a few in the Pacific Ocean

CONSERVATION STATUS
endangered; many deaths due to drowning as accidental bycatch in longline fisheries

BODY SIZE
length
87 cm (34 in)
weight
3.5 kg (7.7 lb)
wingspan
2.5 m (8 ft)

LIFESPAN
40+ years

DIET
fish, squid, krill

BREEDING
arrival
September/October
clutch size
1
incubation
68 days
fledging
4 months

Black-browed albatrosses are the albatrosses most commonly seen by visitors to the Antarctic Peninsula. They often follow ships, and their white head and rump, separated by a dark wing and back, makes them easily distinguished from the giant petrels that are also common behind ships. Black-brows are commonly seen south of the Antarctic Convergence and are even found in the relatively sheltered waters of the fiords of Tierra del Fuego in Argentina and Chile.

As with all albatrosses, juvenile black-brows spend their first few years at sea and do not return to the breeding colonies until they are about five years old. For the next few years they are merely observers: actual breeding doesn't begin until they are about eight years old.

Like other albatrosses, black-brows have elaborate courtship displays that involve many different postures and vocalisations. Successful pairs often stick together for many consecutive breeding seasons and re-use the same nest. These tall, pedestal-like structures are made of peaty soil, grass and mud.

Black-browed albatrosses feed primarily on krill, but also take some fish, squid and salp (a small floating gelatinous animal). Most prey are seized by birds sitting on the water, although some are also taken by surface-plunging and diving to shallow depths.

birds

SCIENTIFIC NAME
Thalassarche chrysostoma

POPULATION SIZE
99,000 breeding pairs

DISTRIBUTION
subantarctic

CONSERVATION STATUS
vulnerable (population
decreasing)

BODY SIZE
length
up to 85 cm (33.5 in)
weight
up to 3.7 kg (8.2 lbs)
wingspan
205 cm (81 in)

DIET
mainly fish and squid

BREEDING
arrival
late September
clutch size
1
incubation
73 days
fledging
141 days

Although large numbers of grey-headed albatrosses feed in the Southern Ocean, they are not conspicuous ship-followers and so good sightings may take some effort. In the south Atlantic they breed on the Diego Ramirez Islands in the Drake Passage, and the 48,000 pairs nesting on South Georgia make up almost half of the world breeding population. They also breed on Campbell and Macquarie Islands in the south Pacific, and in the Indian Ocean on Kerguelen, Crozet and Marion Islands. Grey-headed albatrosses travel widely to feed, usually remaining in subantarctic waters. Satellite tracking of birds from South Georgia has shown some individuals circumnavigating the globe in as little as 46 days.

Like other albatrosses, the grey-headed lays only one egg. However, it differs from other similar sized species in that it usually breeds every second year: a pair that successfully rears a chick will not breed the following season. This unusual timing is a reflection of diet. Grey-headed albatrosses feed mostly on squid, which provides relatively little nutrition. As a result, the chicks grow more slowly and take longer to fledge. Grey-headed albatrosses do not begin breeding until they are ten to 14 years old, making them one of the bird species that defers breeding the longest. The current old-age record is 46 years.

The population of this species has declined alarmingly in recent decades because of competition with commercial fisheries for squid stocks. Grey-headed albatrosses are also prone to being accidentally caught by hooks used for long-line fishing. They follow fishing boats because of the scraps dumped overboard, and frequently mistake the baited hooks for prey. They swallow the hook and are then pulled under and drowned. Their biennial breeding regime makes for a low birth rate, so they are particularly vulnerable to increased mortality resulting from this fisheries' bycatch.

birds

SCIENTIFIC NAME
Phoebetria palpebrata

POPULATION SIZE
22,000 breeding pairs

DISTRIBUTION
circumpolar in Antarctic
and subantarctic latitudes

CONSERVATION STATUS
near-threatened; many
deaths due to drowning
as accidental bycatch in
longline fisheries

BODY SIZE
85 cm (33 in)
weight
3 kg (6.6 lb)
wingspan
2.2m (7.2 ft)

LIFESPAN
32+ years

DIET
squid, fish, carrion

BREEDING
arrival
October
clutch size
1
incubation
68 days
fledging
5 months

The light-mantled sooty albatross is an elegant flier, with tapered wings and a pointy tail not seen in other species. Unlike other albatrosses that visit the Antarctic Peninsula region, it has a dark body everywhere except its paler back – hence the name. It is the only albatross known to breed in Antarctica, with just a few nests found on King George Island.

The light-mantled sooty, and its close relative the sooty albatross, differ from the other albatrosses in several other ways as well. The courtship of most albatrosses takes place firmly on the ground, but the sooties conduct aerial displays, with male and female partners flying in synchrony while calling. Light-mantled sooty albatrosses are also more likely than other species to dive for their food, and depths of up to 9 m (29 ft) have been recorded.

Sooties are keen scavengers. Their diet contains carrion such as penguins and small petrels; the latter are sometimes swallowed whole. Despite their scavenging habits, however, light-mantled sooties rarely follow ships, so it is unusual to see individual birds gliding past.

birds

SCIENTIFIC NAME
Diomedea epomophora
and *D. sanfordi*

POPULATION SIZE
21,500 breeding pairs

DISTRIBUTION
circumpolar in subantarctic
latitudes; breeds only in
New Zealand

CONSERVATION STATUS
vulnerable; many
deaths due to drowning
as accidental bycatch in
longline fisheries

BODY SIZE
length
115 cm (45 in)
weight
9 kg (20 lb)
wingspan
up to 3.5 m (11.5 ft)

LIFESPAN
60+ years

DIET
squid, fish, salps

BREEDING
once every 2 years
arrival
November/December
clutch size
1
incubation
79 days
fledging
8 months

The royal albatrosses and their close relatives the wandering albatrosses have the longest wingspans of any bird species, reaching up to 3.5 m (11.5 ft). Their long, narrow wings are well-suited to efficient flight in the open ocean, where wind is plentiful and obstacles are few, and they spend most of their lives at sea. Aeronautical engineers have copied the albatross's wing design when making gliders.

Royal albatrosses don't begin breeding until they are at least nine years old. Breeding is biennial because it takes more than 12 months to mate and raise a chick. With such a low reproductive rate, royal albatrosses are particularly susceptible to fisheries mortality and, as with wandering albatrosses, the increased use of longline fishing practices has led to a dramatic increase in the number killed as a bycatch.

Royal albatrosses breed only in New Zealand: the northern royal on the Chatham Islands, with an additional small colony of around 20 pairs on New Zealand's South Island mainland; and the southern royal on the subantarctic Campbell and Auckland Islands. They forage around the globe, flying many thousands of kilometres a year, and many juvenile birds are seen in waters near southern South America. Their main prey is squid, although fish, crustaceans and salps are also eaten. Most prey is taken by surface-seizing and, rarely, plunge-diving.

Royal albatrosses can be very long-lived: one female that was banded as an adult lived to be at least 61.

birds

SCIENTIFIC NAME
Diomedea exulans

POPULATION SIZE
**20,000 breeding pairs
(including all species)**

DISTRIBUTION
**circumpolar in
subantarctic latitudes**

CONSERVATION STATUS
**vulnerable; many deaths
due to drowning as
accidental bycatch in
longline fisheries**

BODY SIZE
length
122 cm (48 in)
weight
9 kg (20 lb)
wingspan
up to 3.5 m (11.5 ft)

LIFESPAN
40+ years

DIET
squid, fish, carrion

BREEDING
once every 2 years
arrival
November/December
clutch size
1
incubation
68–79 days
fledging
10–11 months

The wandering albatrosses and their close relatives the royal albatrosses have the longest wingspans of any bird species, reaching up to 3.5 m (11.5 ft). There are five different species of wandering albatross, each taking its specific name from the region in which it breeds. While the birds' plumages vary, their breeding biology is quite similar. The birds pictured here breed on South Georgia and are the type most likely to be seen in the south Atlantic Ocean.

The wandering albatross's long narrow wings are well suited to efficient flight in the open ocean, where wind is plentiful and obstacles few. Satellite-tracking has found that the birds cover vast distances while foraging, and one individual is recorded to have flown over 33,000 km (20,505 miles) in 71 days. They routinely cover more distance in a day than do most cruise ships.

Wandering albatrosses don't begin breeding until they are 10 to 12 years old, and usually remain with the same mate for many years. Because it takes more than 13 months to raise a chick, breeding occurs only every two years. Such a low reproductive rate makes the wandering albatross population particularly susceptible to fisheries mortality, and the increased use of longline fishing practices in the Southern Ocean has led to a dramatic increase in albatross deaths.

Wandering albatrosses feed mainly on squid and fish, plus some crustaceans. Most prey are taken by surface-seizing, although some surface-plunging and pursuit-plunging has been reported.

Antarctic petrel chick moulting its down

SCIENTIFIC NAME
Thalassoica antarctica

POPULATION SIZE
5 million+ breeding pairs
(estimate)

DISTRIBUTION
circumpolar in Antarctic
latitudes, seen most often
in pack-ice zone

CONSERVATION STATUS
least concern

BODY SIZE
length
42 cm (16 in)
weight
675 g (1.5 lb)
wingspan
105 cm (41 in)

DIET
krill, squid, fish

BREEDING
arrival
October
clutch size
1
incubation
46 days
fledging
45 days

Antarctic petrels are seldom seen outside Antarctic waters, and all their breeding sites are south of the Antarctic Convergence. Care must be taken not to confuse them with the similarly coloured Cape petrel. In the Antarctic petrel, the leading edge of the wing, as seen from above, is dark brown-black, while the trailing half of the wing is white. In the Cape petrel the two colours are mixed together in a series of speckles.

Antarctic petrels are also more likely to be found over pack ice, and they frequently roost on icebergs. Flocks of several thousand are sometimes seen flying high in the sky at the completion of the breeding season, although the details of their movements and possible migration are not well-known.

They breed in densely packed colonies with nests less than 1m (3.2 ft) apart. Some large colonies have more than 200,000 pairs. Most colonies are in snow-free areas such as crevices and ledges on sloping coastal rocky cliffs, but large groups have been found nesting 200 km (124 miles) inland.

Antarctic petrels eat crustaceans such as krill and isopods, plus squid and small fish. They catch most of their food by seizing it while sitting on the surface, but have also been observed to dive to depths of 1.5 m (5 ft), using their half-extended wings to 'fly' underwater.

SCIENTIFIC NAME
Daption capense

POPULATION SIZE
100,000+ breeding pairs

DISTRIBUTION
circumpolar in Antarctic
and subantarctic latitudes;
avoids pack ice

CONSERVATION STATUS
least concern

BODY SIZE
length
35 cm (13.8 in)
weight
440 g (1 lb)
wingspan
85 cm (33 in)

LIFESPAN
30+ years

DIET
krill, squid, fish

BREEDING
arrival
October
clutch size
1
incubation
45 days
fledging
48 days

birds

The Cape petrel is an almost constant companion
during an Antarctic cruise, and small flocks will often
follow ships for many hours. One marked bird was
observed to follow a ship for 2400 km (1491 miles).

These birds are found both north and south of the
Antarctic Convergence. They are also known as
pintado petrels, from the Spanish word meaning
'painted', as the tops of their wings appear to have
been splattered with paint drops from a well-laden
brush. They can be confused with the less often seen
Antarctic petrel, but in that species the black and
white portions of the wings are solid colour blocks,
not randomly mixed speckles.

Cape petrels feed on whatever is available, with krill
making up the largest proportion of their diet. They
get most of their food by surface-seizing but can also
be seen swimming in tight circles as they use their feet
to stir food up to the surface.

Breeding doesn't start until age six and most birds keep
the same mate for successive breeding seasons. The
same nest site is used year after year. Like most petrels,
the incubating adult or growing chick will sometimes
repel intruders by vomiting a fishy stomach oil on them
with astonishing accuracy.

SCIENTIFIC NAME
Pagodroma nivea

POPULATION SIZE
63,000+ pairs

DISTRIBUTION
circumpolar in Antarctic
latitudes; seen most
often in pack-ice zone

CONSERVATION STATUS
least concern

BODY SIZE
length
35 cm (13.8 in)
weight
240–460 g (0.5–1 lb)
wingspan
75–95 cm (29–37 in)

DIET
krill, fish, squid,
carrion

BREEDING
arrival
late October/
early November
clutch size
1
incubation
44 days
fledging
48 days

The snow petrel breeds further south than any other
bird species in the world, with some pairs nesting as
far as 300 km (186 miles) inland from the Antarctic
coast. Here they nest in rock crevices on mountains
that stick up through the interior ice sheet at 80°44′S
latitude, only 1049 km (652 miles) from the South
Pole. However, most snow petrels breed in coastal
areas, where they make their nests in narrow crevices
and small caves, which provide some protection from
predatory skuas.

The only all-white petrel in the world, snow petrels
are seldom seen anywhere outside Antarctic waters,
and even here they are usually confined to areas of
pack ice. They do not follow ships but will often fly
in close if one crosses their path. They may be seen
in the company of cape or Antarctic petrels, and it
is not unusual to find them roosting on icebergs.

Snow petrels feed on krill and other pelagic (open
water) crustaceans such as copepods and isopods,
squid and small fish. Most of their food is grabbed
by dipping their heads in the water, but their buoyant
flight makes it possible for some prey to be seized from
the surface without alighting. They are opportunistic
feeders and will eat scraps of food from ships, seal
carcasses, whale blubber and even the dead bodies
of other snow petrels.

Southern giant petrel

SCIENTIFIC NAME
Macronectes giganteus

POPULATION SIZE
60,000

DISTRIBUTION
circumpolar; breeds in Antarctica and subantarctic islands; at sea, found from Antarctica to sub-tropical waters

CONSERVATION STATUS
least concern

BODY SIZE
length
92 cm (36 in)
weight
male – 5 kg (11 lb)
female – 3.8 kg (8.4 lb)
wingspan
up to 2.1 m (6.8 ft)

LIFESPAN
26+ years

DIET
carrion (sea birds, seals, whales), squid, fish, krill

BREEDING
year-round resident
nest building
late October
clutch size
1
incubation
61 days
fledging
117 days

Southern giant petrels are the birds most likely to be seen following ships in the far south. Sometimes referred to as the vultures of the Southern Ocean, they have massive, prehistoric-looking beaks. They have an excellent sense of smell, which they use to locate food, and their habit of feeding on the carcasses of dead seals, birds and even whales generally means they aren't the most popular species seen on a trip to Antarctica.

Despite their fearsome appearance, giant petrels are very easily frightened when approached. Nesting birds, particularly, should be given a wide berth (at least 50 m, or 164 ft). They nest in loose colonies, and, as with all petrels, males and females share the parental duties. They defend their nests tenaciously, using their strong bill and their ability to vomit prodigious volumes of partially digested food and stomach oil at intruders. Their aim is accurate to at least 1 m (3.2 ft).

Male and female giant petrels look alike. Their thick, chunky appearance in flight distinguishes them from the similar-sized albatrosses with which they may be seen at sea. Two different adult plumage forms are known: the dark morph (top left), which is light grey with a pale head, and the white morph (bottom left), which is all white.

The birds breed in Antarctica and on adjacent islands but their numbers are decreasing and the species is considered vulnerable. They are often killed by getting caught on the hooks of longline fishing boats. Human disturbance at nesting colonies is also a factor in their reduced population.

birds

SCIENTIFIC NAME
Procellaria aequinoctialis

POPULATION SIZE
7 million

DISTRIBUTION
subantarctic

CONSERVATION STATUS
vulnerable; population
declining

BODY SIZE
length
up to 58 cm (23 in)
weight
1.39 kg (3.1 lbs)
wingspan
147 cm (58 in)

DIET
fish, squid, crustaceans;
occasional tunicates

BREEDING
arrival
September
clutch size
1
incubation
59 days
fledging
96 days

The white chin is probably the last thing a birdwatcher will see on this sea bird. Instead, note the uniform dark brown or blackish plumage and the strong, slow wing beats. Most birds do indeed have a small patch of white feathers just under the bill, but this is difficult to see from the deck of a ship. Early mariners called this species the 'shoemaker' or 'cobbler', since the calls from the burrows reminded them of the hammering of a shoemaker.

White-chinned petrels breed on most of the subantarctic islands in the Pacific and Indian Oceans, although South Georgia is their stronghold. They range widely in search of food, and satellite tracking has shown them to have the longest average foraging range of any animal – up to 3495 km (2172 miles) from the breeding island.

The birds suffer predation by rats on some islands, but can apparently co-exist with this introduced predator. On islands where cats have been introduced, predation is much higher, and on some of them white-chinned petrels are now extinct. Because they feed aggressively during both nights and days, this species also suffers the highest rates of incidental mortality from trawl and longline fisheries of any species: the birds fly into wire warps and break their wings, or ingest baited hooks and are drowned. Despite a population estimated at seven million pairs, the white-chinned petrel is classified as vulnerable because its numbers are rapidly declining.

SCIENTIFIC NAME
Oceanites oceanicus

POPULATION SIZE
millions of breeding pairs

DISTRIBUTION
breeds in Antarctic and
subantarctic latitudes;
migrates to North Atlantic,
Indian and southern
Pacific Oceans in
non-breeding season

CONSERVATION STATUS
least concern

BODY SIZE
length
17 cm (7 in)
weight
35 g (1 oz)
wingspan
40 cm (15 in)

DIET
krill, amphipods, fish,
carrion

BREEDING
arrival
October
clutch size
1
incubation
45 days
fledging
60 days

Weighing only slightly more than a sparrow, the tiny Wilson's storm petrel is the smallest bird found in Antarctica. Named for the Scottish-born American ornithologist Alexander Wilson, it is also one of the most prolific species in the world – and the most wide-ranging, spending the summer breeding season in Antarctic and subantarctic waters, then moving north of the equator during the austral winter.

The birds sustain themselves on these long migrations by feeding on a wide variety of prey near the surface. Small crustaceans such as amphipods, krill, marine worms and carrion are all part of this generalist's diet, and most of its food is taken while hovering with its feet pattering on the surface. The impression is that the birds are walking on the water. Indeed, the name 'petrel' is derived from the biblical story of St Peter walking on water.

Wilson's storm petrels nest in small crevices in cliffs or between the rocks on talus slopes, where they are protected from predators such as skuas and kelp gulls. Foraging birds return to their breeding sites in the evening, circling the vicinity of their nests many times before finally landing and scurrying down the appropriate crevice. They do not walk easily, moving awkwardly on their lower legs and knees.

SCIENTIFIC NAME
Puffinus griseus

POPULATION SIZE
3 million+ breeding pairs

DISTRIBUTION
circumpolar in sub-
antarctic latitudes;
usually seen north of
Antarctic Convergence

CONSERVATION STATUS
near-threatened

BODY SIZE
length
43 cm (17 in)
weight
800 g (1.7 lb)
wingspan
100 cm (39 in)

DIET
squid, fish, crustaceans

BREEDING
arrival
September/October
clutch size
1
incubation
53 days
fledging
97 days

Sooty shearwaters are often seen in large flocks or, if they are sitting on the water, as 'rafts' in the South Atlantic and Pacific Oceans. While most of the world's population nests in New Zealand, there are sizeable colonies on the islands around Cape Horn and in the Falkland Islands.

Like most petrels, sooty shearwaters dig underground burrows in which to lay their eggs. These provide protection from the extremes of weather, as well as from predators such as skuas and kelp gulls. Humans are another predator and the nearly grown chicks are still eaten today in southern New Zealand.

Sooty shearwaters feed largely on small fish and squid, which they capture just below the surface. However, especially in the area of the Antarctic Convergence, they are known to dive to 68 m (223 ft), 'flying' underwater with their wings only partially open.

Although they breed on subantarctic islands and forage in latitudes ranging as far south as 65°S, sooty shearwaters make long migrations to spend the southern winter months of May to August in the northern hemisphere – in the seas off Japan, Alaska and California, and in the North Atlantic. They fly across the entire Pacific in a figure-of-eight pattern and cover an astonishing 64,000 km (nearly 40,000 miles). This is the longest animal migration ever measured.

SCIENTIFIC NAME
Fulmarus glacialoides

POPULATION SIZE
1.1 million+ breeding pairs

DISTRIBUTION
circumpolar in Antarctic
latitudes; in open water
and pack ice

CONSERVATION STATUS
least concern

BODY SIZE
length
48 cm (19 in)
weight
750 g (1.6 lb)
wingspan
117 cm (46 in)

DIET
krill, squid, fish

BREEDING
arrival
October
clutch size
1
incubation
45 days
fledging
52 days

Although at first glance the southern fulmar resembles a gull, its presence in the open ocean far from any coast, and its habit of gliding only a few centimetres above the surface of the water, are evidence that it is a type of petrel.

Fulmars nest in loose colonies on cliffs and rocky outcrops on the Antarctic mainland and nearby islands. In the peninsula region their breeding headquarters are the northernmost part of the South Shetlands (the Elephant Island group), the South Orkneys and the South Sandwich Islands. Nests are usually north-facing so the sun melts away the snow, but the birds also use their bills to shovel away deeper accumulations.

Fulmars feed on fish, krill and squid, the proportions varying with the season and region. As heavy fliers that cannot remain aloft at slow speeds, they do not dip-feed while on the wing but usually land on the surface before seizing their prey. When krill is concentrated, large flocks of fulmars and other petrels will be seen crowded together, taking advantage of the easy pickings. However, when the food bonanza is carrion – for example, a dead seal – the fulmars are conspicuously absent from the feeding mêlée.

SCIENTIFIC NAME
Pachyptila desolata

POPULATION SIZE
50 million

DISTRIBUTION
subantarctic and Antarctica

CONSERVATION STATUS
least concern

BODY SIZE
length
27 cm (11 in)
weight
160 g (5.6 oz)
wingspan
66 cm (26 in)

DIET
krill & other crustaceans;
small quantities of fish &
squid

BREEDING
arrival
mid October
clutch size
1
incubation
45
fledging
51 days

One of the most common birds in Antarctic waters is also one of the hardest to see. The Antarctic prion exists in large flocks, but its erratic flying, cryptic colouration, and tendency to stay close to the water make viewing it difficult. The grey-blue of the top of the birds' wings blends with the colour of the sea. Hence, prions are most conspicuous when turning as this exposes the white underside.

The Antarctic prion is one of seven species of prion found in the Southern Ocean. All are similar in appearance and only the most experienced birders can identify them at sea. Some species require bill measurements for identification. The name 'prion' is from the Greek word for saw, a reference to the lamellae, or fine plates, on the edge of the bill, which act as a sieve. Early sailors knew them as whalebirds or dove-petrels and the dainty, elegant look of these birds makes the latter name particularly apt.

Prions feed on small crustaceans such as krill, copepods and amphipods. Most prey is gathered by surface seizing, where the bird alights on the water and grabs food items while sitting. Prions also have a unique feeding technique known as hydroplaning, where they use their feet to propel themselves along the surface, with their beak and head underwater. In this way they filter small prey from the water using the lamellae on the edge of the upper beak.

SCIENTIFIC NAME
Phalacrocorax bransfieldensis

POPULATION SIZE
c.10,000 breeding pairs on Antarctic Peninsula

DISTRIBUTION
Antarctic Peninsula and South Shetland Islands

CONSERVATION STATUS
least concern, but some populations declining

BODY SIZE
length
77 cm (30 in)
weight
3 kg (6.6 lb)
wingspan
94 cm (37 in)

DIET
fish, some bottom-dwelling crustaceans

DIVING BEHAVIOUR
maximum depth
113 m (372 ft)
maximum duration
5.3 minutes

BREEDING
resident year-round
nesting begins
October
clutch size
2–3
incubation
30 days
fledging
65 days

The only shag (cormorant) found in Antarctica, at a distance the Antarctic shag is sometimes mistaken for a penguin. There is a superficial resemblance in the upright stance and black and white pattern, but the shag has a longer neck, often with a visible curve. The shag's ability to fly also clearly separates the two species. The Antarctic shag is also known as the blue-eyed shag, but the apparent blueness of its eyes is really a ring of deep blue skin around the eye. Males occasionally make a bark-like noise, but female vocalisations are limited to hissing, and seldom heard.

The diving ability of this species is astounding, outstripping that of any other flying bird in Antarctica, and rivalling that of some of the penguins. It is known to dive to 113 m (371 ft), while the similarly sized chinstrap penguin dives to 102 m (334 ft). And unlike the supremely adapted penguin, which moves through the water with powerful flipper-strokes, the shag propels itself with just its webbed feet. Females dive significantly deeper than males.

Shag nests – conspicuous conical bowls made of seaweed, moulted feathers and even dead shags, all cemented together with wet excrement – are perhaps the most elaborate of any species in Antarctica. Both sexes help build the nest: males collect the marine algae by diving and then flying back with large tufts of it sticking out of their bills, while females do most of the actual construction. After hatching, both sexes feed the chicks, which continue to get parental hand-outs after fledging. Breeding success varies widely from one season to the next, but overall it has been declining in the peninsula in the past decade, with several colonies shrinking dramatically. Similar species and subspecies are found in the Falkland Islands, Tierra del Fuego and other subantarctic islands.

birds

SCIENTIFIC NAME
Larus dominicanus

POPULATION SIZE
1 million+ breeding pairs
worldwide

DISTRIBUTION
circumpolar in temperate
and subantarctic
latitudes, plus the
Antarctic Peninsula
and nearby islands

CONSERVATION STATUS
least concern

BODY SIZE
length
59 cm (23 in)
weight
1.2 kg (2.6 lb)
wingspan
135 cm (53 in)

DIET
In Antarctica: limpets
Elsewhere: eggs and
chicks of other birds,
carrion

BREEDING
arrival
October
clutch size
2–3
incubation
27 days
fledging
49 days

Worldwide, the kelp gull is one of the most widespread gulls but it is the only species of gull to occur in Antarctica. It is commonly seen on the Antarctic Peninsula (to about 68°S), the South Shetland Islands, South Orkneys, South Sandwich, South Georgia, the Falklands and the mainland of South America. Elsewhere in the world it is commonly associated with cities and farms, which produce the rubbish on which such a generalist feeder can live well.

Unlike petrels, kelp gulls are not found in the open ocean; they are coastal birds. In Antarctica, they do not prey on the eggs and chicks of their neighbours, as is common in more temperate areas. Rather, their diet consists almost exclusively of limpets, and their distribution is closely tied to that of this intertidal mollusc. Kelp gulls swallow the limpet whole, digest its fleshy foot and then regurgitate the shell. Kelp gull colonies are usually full of middens of these discarded shells.

The birds lay two to three eggs in a nest that is often just a shallow scrape, sometimes built up with a bit of lichen or moss.

The kelp gull is one of the few species of bird to remain in the Antarctic Peninsula during the winter.

SCIENTIFIC NAME
Catharacta lonnbergi and
C. maccormicki

POPULATION SIZE
5000–8000 breeding pairs

DISTRIBUTION
subantarctic islands and
Antarctic coastlines

CONSERVATION STATUS
least concern

BODY SIZE
length
53 cm (20 in)
weight
c. 1.1 kg (2.4 lb)
wingspan
143 cm (56 in)

LIFESPAN
20+ years

DIET
fish, penguins' eggs and
chicks, carrion

BREEDING
arrival
mid November
clutch size
2
incubation
c. 30 days
fledging
55 days

Skuas are conspicuous residents of many parts of Antarctica. However, their bold flying and curious nature give the impression they are more common than they really are. Skuas will fly in close to investigate cruise ships, often hovering over the deck while inspecting the activity below. On shore they are usually seen around penguin colonies, where they are active predators of eggs and chicks, as well as scavengers on birds that have died of other causes.

Adult penguins have nothing to fear from skuas. Indeed, penguins will sometimes attack a skua. When caught, the skua will certainly come off second-best, being less than 20 percent the weight of the penguin. Penguin chicks, however, are frequently taken, usually after they have grown large enough for an adult not to be guarding them. A skua that has captured a penguin chick often attracts the attention of other skuas and then has to fight to keep control of its meal. Such behaviour makes it hard for some people to love skuas, but they are, of course, just as important a part of the ecosystem as penguins.

Skuas vigorously defend their nests from intruders, whether human, or other skuas, issuing loud alarm calls and even dive-bombing to chase the intruder past their territorial boundary. If you are strafed by a skua while ashore, you are obviously too close to the nest. Retrace your steps and quickly leave the area. During all the commotion the chicks will usually remain motionless on the ground. Take care not to step on them.

Ornithologists are still debating the scientific classification of skua. Traditionally, two species are described as living in the Antarctic Peninsula but some scientists consider these to be different races of the same species, and hybridisation does occur. For the non-specialist, their similarities outnumber their differences and so they are simply treated here as 'skuas'.

SCIENTIFIC NAME
Sterna vittata

POPULATION SIZE
c. 50,000 breeding pairs

DISTRIBUTION
circumpolar in
subantarctic latitudes,
plus Antarctic Peninsula
and nearby islands

CONSERVATION STATUS
least concern

BODY SIZE
length
36 cm (14 in)
weight
160 g (0.3 lb)
wingspan
77 cm (30 in)

DIET
small fish, krill and
other crustaceans

BREEDING
arrival
resident year-round
clutch size
1–2 (rarely 3)
incubation
24 days
fledging
25 days

Terns fly in a way that is best described as dainty and buoyant, with strong wing-beats and little gliding. Their generally pale appearance means they are sometimes mistaken for snow petrels, but the presence of a black cap and bright red beak confirms a tern.

Antarctic terns are the most commonly seen terns in Antarctic waters, although Arctic terns are also present in summer months. This much-vaunted master of migration breeds in the Arctic, then comes to Antarctica during the northern winter; if you see an Arctic tern, it will be in winter plumage, with a white forehead and a black bill.

Terns have a very light wing-loading, meaning they weigh very little compared to the size of their wings. This gives them excellent control at slow speeds, which in turn allows them to grab small fish, copepods and krill from the surface of the water without getting more than their faces wet. Windy conditions make it easier for terns to hover over a prey item, but if the wind is too strong it ruffles the surface of the water and makes it difficult for terns to spot their food. Prey beneath the surface is reached by plunge-diving, with the tern dropping into the water from a height of several metres.

Terns feed their chicks with food that is whole, not partially digested and regurgitated like the food of most other sea birds, and foraging is usually done close to the nest. The nest is not much more than a scrape, and chicks three or more days old usually leave this spot to hide among the rocks when their parents are away foraging. They return to the scrape to be fed or brooded. Parents continue to feed and defend their chicks for some time after the chicks have fledged or learned to fly.

SCIENTIFIC NAME
Chionis alba

POPULATION SIZE
c. 10,000 breeding pairs

DISTRIBUTION
breeds on Antarctic
Peninsula, South
Shetlands, South Orkneys,
South Georgia; also non-
breeders on Falkland
Islands and Tierra
del Fuego

CONSERVATION STATUS
least concern

BODY SIZE
length
37 cm (14 in)
weight
620 g (1.4 lb)
wingspan
77 cm (30 in)

DIET
penguin and shag eggs
and chicks; krill and fish
stolen from penguins;
seal and bird excrement

BREEDING
resident year-round
nesting
October/ November
clutch size
2–3
incubation
30 days
fledging
55 days

Sheathbills are the only Antarctic birds that do not get their food directly from the sea. Rather, they feed off penguins and shags as predators, scavengers and thieves.

Around the colonies of other birds, sheathbills prey on eggs and small chicks by quickly dashing in to grab their prize, while dodging the powerful bills of the protective adults. As penguin chicks grow they become too large for the sheathbill to tackle, and this is when the birds switch to thievery. A sheathbill will rush in and disrupt an adult penguin as it feeds its chick by regurgitation. This results in the pre-digested krill or fish spilling on the ground, where the penguins no longer recognise it as food. The sheathbill then scoops it up and has an easy meal.

In the winter, when there are no eggs or chicks on which to prey, sheathbills make do on a diet of bird and seal excrement.

The only Antarctic birds without webbed feet, sheathbills are quick on their feet. While their running about brings to mind pigeons or chickens, they are not closely related to either, and it is thought that the gulls may be their nearest relatives. Cheeky and unafraid of people, sheathbills will investigate rucksacks and other equipment you leave unattended.

Gentoo penguin

Penguins

If there is one animal for which people come to Antarctica, it's the penguin. Penguin sightings are a highlight of any Antarctic cruise, whether you are viewing them from the deck of the ship or going ashore to walk among them.

Chinstrap penguin

BODY FORM

Although their very ancient ancestors were flying birds, penguins have evolved as specialised divers and swimmers, and have had their present form for the last 45 million years. Scientifically, they make up the order *Sphenisciformes*. The word means 'little wedge-shaped', a reference to the shape of their wings. Penguins' wings are so small they are usually called flippers.

As underwater specialists, penguins have several features that make them different from what most of us think of as birds. Most birds' bones are filled with air chambers and therefore light in weight, making it easier for the birds to get off the ground. Penguin bones do not have these air cavities and are therefore much heavier, so it is easier for these birds to dive underwater. And the penguin body, although bulky, is streamlined to minimise drag in the viscous water where the birds will spend most of their lives.

Penguins 'fly' through water using the same wing-beats and muscles other birds use for flying through air. Their flippers provide the power while their webbed feet, tucked in under their tail, are used for steering.

Penguins are also different when it comes to feathers. Whereas most birds have feathers which grow in lines, with gaps of featherless skin in between, penguin feathers cover all the skin, just like the fur on a hamster's back. These densely packed feathers provide an impregnable coat that prevents water from reaching the skin, and enables the bird to stay warm in cold water. The feathers themselves are short and stiff, with lots of down at the base.

Emperor penguin

These dense feathers, together with a layer of blubber under the skin, do an excellent job of conserving a penguin's body heat, even in a blizzard. However, the same features prevent the penguin from warming its chicks or eggs with body heat. Fortunately, though, penguins have a brood patch, a special break in their 'defences' that allows heat to escape in just the right spot. The brood patch is a tiny patch of pink skin on the belly of both males and females – a gap in the feathery armour against which the eggs or chicks can nestle.

The general colouration of penguins is black on the back and white underneath. Known as countershading, this provides effective camouflage against predators such as the leopard seal when swimming through water. Seen from below, the penguin's white belly merges with the bright water surface, and seen from above its black back merges with the dark ocean depths.

Moulting Adélie chick

Penguins do not moult their feathers gradually like other birds, but do so in one 2 to 3 week period, when they come ashore and sit still while the new feathers grow and push out the old quills. During this time the birds are not waterproof, so they remain on shore, fasting, until the process is complete. Moulting penguins look very shaggy and unkempt, but they are perfectly healthy. It is important to avoid disturbing them since their fat reserves provide barely enough energy for changing feathers. If a bird is forced to move much to avoid visitors, it may not have sufficient reserves to finish the moult successfully.

Adélie penguin

BEHAVIOUR

Antarctic penguins all nest in colonies, where their breeding is synchronised. This means that within any particular colony most eggs are laid around the same time, hatch around the same time, and the chicks develop at the same pace. The only exceptions are when some penguins lay eggs in higher areas where the snow melts first: these eggs will hatch days earlier than those in the lower places.

Chinstrap penguin

Male and female penguins both take an active role in raising the chicks. Both sexes incubate the eggs (except in the case of the emperor penguin, where only males incubate), feed the chicks, and guard the nest. This shared labour is so important that a penguin chick will not survive if it has only one parent. Chicks that lose a parent to a predator are doomed to starvation, or to becoming prey themselves.

Gentoo penguins with skua

Life in a penguin colony (sometimes called a rookery) is noisy and dirty, with adults calling and displaying to one another, chicks squeaking as they beg for food, and birds commuting from sea to nest with the latest delivery of meals. Chicks who are hungry will beg from any adult penguin, but there is no fostering and adults will feed only their own offspring, whom they recognise by their distinctive calls. Visitors may also witness skuas or snowy sheathbills stalking penguin chicks, trying to secure a meal for their own growing brood. Take the time to sit and observe, and the richness of this busy place will be revealed.

Antarctic penguin species
- Adélie
- Emperor
- Macaroni
- Chinstrap
- Gentoo

IDENTIFICATION

Penguins are the easiest species of wildlife to identify in Antarctica, all having highly recognisable colouration. The head is the key, as this differs in each species. Size is difficult to determine in the open expanse of Antarctica, so identification will require you to see the head of the penguin.

Emperor penguin

Wingless divers

'Wingless diver' is how the scientific name of the emperor penguin (*Aptenodytes*) translates. This is the largest species of penguin, but unless the birds are standing next to those of another species, or something else by which to judge scale, their size won't be much help. Instead, look for the splash of orange and yellow on the side of the head and the top of the breast: no other Antarctic penguin is as colourful. If you can't see the colour of the bird, check the length of the flippers. In emperors, they are quite short compared to the body length. The emperor's closest relative is the king penguin, found only in the subantarctic islands.

Rump-legged penguins

This group includes the Adélie, chinstrap and gentoo penguins. The genus name, *Pygoscelis*, means 'rump leg' or 'elbow leg'. Sometimes erroneously called the brush-tailed penguins (in reality all penguins, not just these three, swish their tails like brooms), these penguins are the ones most commonly encountered in Antarctica. The gentoo is

easily identified: it's the only penguin with a red beak. The chinstrap has an obvious black line on its white throat, and the simply-patterned Adélie has an all-black face with a white ring of feathers around the eye.

Crested penguins

Widespread in the subantarctic zone, the six species of crested penguins all have bright yellow or orange tassles above their eyes. Their scientific name, *Eudyptes*, means 'true diver'. The only crested penguin found in Antarctica is the macaroni, which is easily identified by the blazing orange plumes that make a crown on its head.

TOP *Gentoo penguin*
LEFT *Macaroni penguin*

birds

Penguin facts
- 18 species worldwide
- only 5 species found in Antarctica
- live only in the southern hemisphere
- no penguins in the Arctic
- evolved from flying birds
- the best divers of all birds
- have the most dense feathering of any bird

birds

SCIENTIFIC NAME
Pygoscelis adeliae

POPULATION SIZE
2.6 million+ pairs
worldwide

DISTRIBUTION
circumpolar within
Antarctic latitudes

CONSERVATION STATUS
least concern

BODY SIZE
height
58 cm (23 in)
weight
5 kg (11 lb)

DIET
krill, fish, squid

DIVING BEHAVIOUR
maximum depth
170 m (560 ft)
maximum duration
6 minutes

BREEDING
arrival
October
clutch size
2 eggs
incubation
35 days
fledging
50 days

When most people try to imagine a typical penguin, the Adélie springs to mind. With its simple black and white pattern and absence of any bright colours, it is a symbol of the far south. The Adélie's breeding range is largely confined to Antarctica, and the bird nests further south than any other penguin. Adélies are sometimes affected by extensive sea-ice cover hindering access to their nesting places, and in some years there has been no breeding at all in the most southerly colonies.

Adélie penguins often forage far from their colonies, and during the incubation phase have been known to travel up to 100 km (62 miles) to feed. Once the chicks hatch and require frequent feeding, these foraging trips are shortened considerably, with many finding food within 12 km (7.4 miles). Adélie penguins favour the feeding conditions found in and around extensive sea ice and near the Antarctic Peninsula; where these conditions have become less common in the past two decades, Adélie populations have declined.

Adélie penguins were often used as food for explorers in the early twentieth century, but because the birds migrate north and spend the winter in the pack ice, many were harvested before they left the colonies. The frozen birds were usually stockpiled outside the huts in stacks, like cordwood.

Adélie penguins

SCIENTIFIC NAME
Pygoscelis antarctica

POPULATION SIZE
7.4 million+ pairs

DISTRIBUTION
most colonies confined
to Antarctic Peninsula
and nearby islands in
the Scotia Arc (South
Shetlands, South Orkneys
and South Sandwiches)

CONSERVATION STATUS
least concern

BODY SIZE
height
59 cm (23 in)
weight
3.8 kg (8.3 lb)

DIET
krill, fish

DIVING BEHAVIOUR
maximum depth
121 m (337 ft)

BREEDING
arrival
October/November
incubation period
35 days
fledging
c. 55 days

Chinstrap penguins take their name from the obvious line of black feathers that runs, like the strap of a hat, under their white chins. Chinstraps are a feisty species, and a visit to one of their colonies is usually a noisy affair. Adults on nests will frequently point their heads skyward and trumpet a call that is thought to be a territorial proclamation. It seems to be contagious, because once one bird begins this ecstatic display his or her neighbours soon copy it, and the cacophony spreads throughout the colony.

Chinstraps feed almost entirely on krill, plus a few fish in inshore waters. Uniquely among penguins, the stomach lining of chinstraps is periodically sloughed off and expelled by vomiting. This may possibly be done to remove the high levels of fluoride that the birds ingest when they eat krill, whose rigid external coverings are rich in this toxic material. Chinstrap populations have expanded in the past century and in some areas they have replaced Adélie penguins as the locally dominant penguin species. It is thought that this is because the warming of the Antarctic Peninsula region in the past century has seen a reduction in sea-ice cover – conditions that favour chinstraps over Adélies.

birds

SCIENTIFIC NAME
Aptenodytes forsteri

POPULATION SIZE
190,000+ breeding pairs

DISTRIBUTION
circumpolar but
restricted to areas
within the limit
of pack ice

CONSERVATION STATUS
least concern, although
some populations are
declining

BODY SIZE
height
90 cm (35 in)
weight
female – 30 kg (66 lb)
male – 38 kg (84 lb)

DIET
fish, squid, krill

DIVING BEHAVIOUR
maximum depth
564 m (1833 ft)
maximum duration
22 minutes

BREEDING
arrival
March/April
incubation
65 days (solely done
by males)
fledging
c. 150 days

Emperor penguins are the largest penguin species alive today, although about 25 million years ago some species were much larger, weighing over 80 kg (178 lb). Emperors are also the best cold-adapted bird in the world. They are unique in that they breed during the Antarctic winter. They also differ from other penguins in that they breed on sea ice, not land; lay only a single egg, not two; cradle the egg on top of their feet instead of building a nest; and have an incubation period of two months, compared with only one month for other Antarctic penguins.

The incubation is done entirely by males. Once the egg is laid, the female departs to feed herself, and does not return until after the egg has hatched. Remarkably, the males go without food for about three months during the coldest weather experienced by any vertebrate animal. In the worst conditions, they huddle together for warmth and protection. Emperors are less aggressive than other penguins and will tolerate close contact with other colony members. When the chicks finally hatch, the adult birds must often walk more than 100 km (62 miles) to reach open water and find food.

Large body size makes for efficient diving, and it is no surprise that emperors are the best divers of all the birds. A maximum depth of 534 m (1833 ft) has been recorded, although most of their foraging dives are much shallower. Adult emperor penguins have no predators while on the ice, but in the water leopard seals and killer whales eat them.

Emperor penguins breed further south than most tour ships go, so unfortunately ship-based visitors seldom see this species.

SCIENTIFIC NAME
Aptenodytes patagonicus

POPULATION SIZE
2 million+ breeding pairs

DISTRIBUTION
subantarctic

CONSERVATION STATUS
least concern

BODY SIZE
height
65–75 cm (25–29 in)
weight
13.4 kg (29.5 lbs)

DIET
small fish (especially
lanternfish), squid

DIVING BEHAVIOUR
maximum depth
320 m (1050 ft)
maximum duration
9 min

BREEDING
arrival
at any time
clutch size
1
incubation
56 days
fledging
c. 50 weeks

King penguins are spectacular birds whose splashy orange feathers and docile nature make them a favourite with visitors. The second biggest penguin species after their close relative the emperor, kings are confined to the subantarctic islands. About 450,000 pairs inhabit South Georgia, with large populations found on Macquarie, Kerguelen and Crozet Islands. A small number also inhabit the Falkland Islands. Adults have bright orange patches while immature birds are a paler yellow. The comma-shaped ear patches are important in the courtship display. Chicks are a uniform brown with down so long and fluffy it looks almost like fur. King penguins of all ages are inquisitive and often approach visitors who remain still and quiet.

Males and females take turns incubating the egg and feeding the chick. Feeding is sometimes infrequent during winter months and the chicks may fast for several weeks. Chick-rearing takes longer than for any other penguin species, with about 14 months between egg-laying and the chick becoming independent. As a result, a breeding pair can raise a maximum of two chicks in three years. This unusual cycle also means that, unlike other penguins, a colony of kings is not synchronised in its breeding. Visitors to a colony will find some birds incubating, some brooding small chicks, and others with large chicks nearing fledging.

King penguins do not build a nest but incubate their single egg by resting it on top of their feet, slouching over it so that the loose skin on their belly wraps it protectively. Birds with eggs and small chicks remain segregated from the hurly-burly of the rest of the colony and visitors should be careful not to get too close as these individuals are quite vulnerable to disturbance. Give a wide berth to any penguin with a prominent 'pot belly'. →

→ Moulting penguins also require extra caution since these scruffy-looking individuals are in the energy-sapping process of growing new feathers. They are not waterproof and so cannot go to sea to feed. Instead, they rely on fat reserves for the three weeks or so that it takes for new feathers to replace the old. Conserving energy is crucial for a moulting penguin, and if it must move to get away from a tourist it burns valuable reserves it needs to complete the moult.

In the nineteenth and twentieth centuries, king penguin numbers dwindled because the birds were used by sealers as a source of fuel and food, and were also commercially harvested. Since then, numbers are believed to have risen back to the level prior to sealing.

SCIENTIFIC NAME
Pygoscelis papua

POPULATION SIZE
317,000 pairs

DISTRIBUTION
Antarctic Peninsula and
nearby islands, Falkland
Islands, South Georgia,
Macquarie Island and
subantarctic islands in
the Indian Ocean

CONSERVATION STATUS
near threatened

BODY SIZE
height
61 cm (24 in)
weight
6 kg (13 lb)

DIET
fish, krill

DIVING BEHAVIOUR
maximum depth
225 m (495 ft)

BREEDING
arrival
September/October
clutch size
2
incubation
35 days
fledging
80 days

The orange-beaked gentoo is commonly seen around the Antarctic Peninsula, although only about 12 percent of the world population is found this far south. As penguins go, gentoos are among the least aggressive. A visit to a gentoo colony reveals that they are not nearly as noisy as their close cousins, the chinstraps or the Adélies.

Gentoos feed on fish and krill close to shore, often within 4 km (2.5 miles) of their nests. In some populations, females eat mostly krill, while males switch between krill and fish.

Male and female birds share incubating and chick-rearing duties. For the first 25 days of a chick's life it will be constantly guarded by one of its parents while the other is away feeding in inshore waters. At 3 to 4 weeks the chicks are big enough to defend themselves, and to keep warm they sometimes huddle together with other chicks in a 'crèche'. At this stage they demand increasing quantities of food, so both parents must forage at the same time. Unusually for penguins, gentoo chicks return to the nesting colony to be fed by their parents for about 3 weeks after fledging.

In winter, gentoos from Antarctic colonies disperse, but they don't truly migrate. Some individuals will even visit their nest sites occasionally. At sea, they avoid pack ice.

Why this penguin is called 'gentoo' is not clear. The word is of Anglo-Indian and Portuguese origin and means a 'pagan inhabitant of Hindustan'. The bird's scientific name, 'papua', is also obscure. It comes from a Malayan word meaning 'curly', but there is nothing obviously curly about a gentoo. Johann Forster, the German naturalist who accompanied James Cook on his second Pacific voyage (1772–75) and did the first formal description, based on specimens collected in the Falkland Islands, may have been confused by an erroneous report that the birds were also found in New Guinea.

SCIENTIFIC NAME
Eudyptes chrysolophus

POPULATION SIZE
11.8 million+
breeding pairs

DISTRIBUTION
mainly in subantarctic
latitudes of the Atlantic
and Indian Oceans,
but some found in
Antarctic Peninsula

CONSERVATION STATUS
vulnerable; some colonies
have decreased markedly
in the past 40 years

BODY SIZE
height
57 cm (22 in)
weight
female – 5 kg (11 lb)
male – 6 kg (12.2 lb)

DIET
krill, fish, squid

DIVING BEHAVIOUR
maximum depth
148 m (396 ft)
maximum duration
6 minutes

BREEDING
arrival
late November
(for Antarctic pairs)
incubation
35 days
fledging
56 days

Although macaroni penguins are the most numerous penguin species in the world, only a small number breed in Antarctica – a few hundred pairs in the peninsula region and about 7000 pairs in the Elephant Island group.

Most of their nests will be found scattered among the colonies of chinstrap penguins, where the bold orange-gold crests of the macaroni make for easy identification in a sea of black and white birds. The name 'macaroni' comes from an eighteenth-century English slang term for a man who dressed in the gaudy, flamboyant style popular in Italy at the time – immortalised in the early American song 'Yankee doodle'.

Like all crested penguins, macaronis lay two eggs, with the first being 40 percent smaller than the second and less likely to hatch. Incubation does not begin properly until the second egg has been laid, by which stage the embryo in the first egg is dead, or at the very least cold. The first egg is usually lost from the nest before the second egg hatches, and only one chick is ever raised per season. This characteristic has puzzled evolutionary biologists since its discovery and there has been considerable debate as to its explanation. The leading theory suggests that we are witnessing an intermediate stage between a 2-egg clutch and a 1-egg clutch.

Macaroni penguins feed mainly on krill, small fish and cephalopods, which they capture by pursuit-diving, mainly in water up to 20 m (66 ft) deep.

SCIENTIFIC NAME
Eudyptes chrysocome

POPULATION SIZE
**850,000 breeding pairs
(declining)**

DISTRIBUTION
subantarctic

CONSERVATION STATUS
vulnerable

BODY SIZE
height
39 cm (15 in)
weight
3.4 kg (7.5 lbs)

DIET
krill, squid, fish

DIVING BEHAVIOUR
maximum depth
110 m (360 ft)
maximum duration
3 min

BREEDING
arrival
August–October
clutch size
2
incubation
33–39 days
fledging
71 days

birds

The smallest of the subantarctic penguins, rockhoppers take their name from their preferred method of locomotion on the steep slopes they inhabit. They are widespread on islands in the Southern Ocean, including the Falklands, Staten Island and the islands near Cape Horn. In the Falkland Islands, rockhoppers often nest in close association with black-browed albatrosses, and their mixed colonies can be seen on Steeple Jason, New and West Point Islands.

Rockhopper nesting sites are usually found along the windward side of these islands. The nests are simple structures of grass, pebbles and peat. As with all crested penguins, the two eggs that rockhoppers lay each season are of different sizes: the first is smaller than the second. While both eggs usually hatch, the chick from the second is most often the only one to survive to fledging.

Rockhoppers were harvested for oil and skins in the nineteenth century, and until recently their eggs were consumed by Falkland Islanders. Despite this, their populations remained high until the middle of the twentieth century. Since then, numbers have dropped by as much as 94 percent on some islands. In the Falklands, the population plummeted over 80 percent between 1933 and 1996, although it seems to have stabilised currently at around 272,000 pairs.

Rockhoppers are truly at home in the water and they spend their winters at sea, not coming ashore for five or six months. Feeding takes place in shallow water over continental shelf areas. In the south-west Atlantic populations, this means foraging takes place between the Falklands and Patagonia.

birds

SCIENTIFIC NAME
Spheniscus magellanicus

POPULATION SIZE
1.3 million breeding pairs

DISTRIBUTION
southern South America;
Falklands

CONSERVATION STATUS
near threatened,
population decreasing

BODY SIZE
height
59 cm (23 in)
weight
4.8 kg (10.6 lbs)

DIET
crustaceans, small fish,
squid

DIVING BEHAVIOUR
maximum depth
91 m (299 ft)
maximum duration
4.6 min

BREEDING
arrival
September
clutch size
2
incubation
40 days
fledging
c. 60–70 days

The Magellanic penguin is the most conspicuous penguin in southern South America. Large colonies can be easily visited at several sites along the coast of southern Argentina, in the Straits of Magellan, and near Punta Arenas in Chile. They also inhabit the Falkland Islands, where modest numbers can be seen on the beaches near Stanley and on outer islands. While the birds breed in these southerly locations, in winter they disperse at sea and it is not uncommon to find Magellanic penguins in Brazil in July and August.

Note the pink areas around the face: this is bare skin that helps prevent overheating when conditions are hot. These featherless areas work as radiators, venting body heat when they are suffused with blood.

Magellanic penguins nest underground in burrows that they dig with their beaks and feet. These burrows, which can be several metres deep, provide protection from predators such as foxes. They also shield the eggs and chicks from the hot, sunny conditions that prevail during summer in Patagonia. Nests are often infested with fleas. Adult penguins use the burrows as a refuge and will dive underground if they feel threatened. At colonies frequently visited by tourists, Magellanic penguins allow a close approach and appear to be unbothered by the presence of people, but where visitors are uncommon they are very skittish, and great care is needed not to drive them underground.

Magellanic penguin populations have declined by 50 to 80 percent since the 1980s, in part due to food shortages caused by intensive commercial fishing activity within their range. They also share their feeding grounds with an expanding oil industry; an estimated 40,000 birds are killed each year by oil spills. Should oil extraction begin in the Falklands (the geology looks promising), this number may increase.

Crabeater seal

Mammals

Southern elephant seal

Seals

Seals are one of the most commonly seen and distinctive animals in Antarctica, often found sleeping on beaches or lazing on ice floes. But don't make the mistake of thinking they're lazy – it's just that we see them only when they're resting. All their feeding activity takes place underwater and out of sight. Also, much of it is conducted during the night.

Seals, sea lions and walruses are all part of a group of marine creatures called the pinnipeds, or 'feather-footed' – carnivorous aquatic mammals that use flippers to move on land and in the water, and spend most of their lives swimming or eating at sea. There are 34 species of pinnipeds, and their habitats range from the Arctic to the Antarctic, from the temperate regions of both hemispheres to the tropics.

Seals can be broadly divided into the phocids, which have no external ear, and the otariids, which have an obvious ear.

Of the six seal species found in Antarctica, four – the Ross, crabeater, leopard and Weddell – inhabit the ice and icy waters that surround the continent and are seldom seen on land. All are confined to Antarctica. The other two species – the Antarctic fur seal and the southern elephant seal – are creatures of the shoreline and seldom encountered in the ice. They are both widespread outside of Antarctica.

mammals

Seal facts
- air-breathing
- mammals with dense fur coats
- come ashore or on to ice to give birth to pups
- nostrils are closed in the 'relaxed' position; they need to contract muscles to open them
- frequently bothered by nasal mites, which lead to runny noses
- Antarctic fur seals and southern elephant seals were hunted almost to extinction in the 1800s. Both species are now fully protected and populations have recovered
- the crabeater seal is the most numerous seal species in the world

Antarctic seal species
- Antarctic fur
- Crabeater
- Leopard
- Ross
- Southern elephant
- Weddell

BODY FORM

As with all aquatic animals that swim fast through water, the body needs to be streamlined. Seals have a fusiform, or cigar-shaped, body, wide in the middle and tapering at the front and back – a shape that reduces drag. Their bodies are also very flexible, so they are able to turn sharply and perform acrobatic movements underwater. Thrust is provided by either the flippers (forelimbs), as in the Antarctic fur seal and other otariids, or by the undulations of the body and hindlimbs, as in the phocids.

Young southern elephant seal

The slit-shaped nostrils of seals are unusual. When the nostrils are relaxed, they remain sealed in the closed position, preventing water from entering the respiratory passages. To take a breath, seals must contract the muscles around the nasal opening. This is highly beneficial for an animal that spends most of its time underwater.

BEHAVIOUR

Compared with seals elsewhere in the world, a high proportion of Antarctic species are specialist feeders on one type of prey. Antarctic fur seals, leopard seals and crabeater seals all make krill the bulk of their diet, and the teeth of leopards and crabeaters in particular are well adapted to sieve krill from the water.

Seals not only spend much of their life in the water, but catch all their food there. Southern elephant seals can dive over 1.6 km (1 mile)

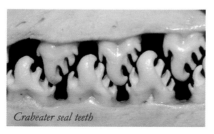

Crabeater seal teeth

beneath the surface to capture fish and squid, and Weddell seals are also known to go almost 800 m (0.5 miles) down. Their ability to operate in a realm of intense cold, no light and crushing pressure is astounding.

Special physiology is required for a mammal to function without breathing for as much as an hour at a time, and the key to success is in storing lots of oxygen and using it conservatively. Seals do not hold their breath when they dive. Instead, most of the oxygen taken in during breathing is stored in their blood and muscles.

The volume of blood in a Weddell seal is 20 percent greater, relative to body size, than that of a human. And not only do seals have more blood than people, their blood can also hold more than three times more oxygen. In addition, seals can drop their heart rate from 100 beats per minute at the surface to fewer than 10 beats per minute when submerged. The greatly reduced blood flow is redirected to service only priority areas such as the brain and heart, thereby lengthening the time the animal can forage underwater.

BREEDING

A non-breeding seal does not have any need to leave the water, for a seal can comfortably rest and sleep at the surface and get all its food from the sea. However, giving birth, known as pupping, requires a solid platform and Antarctic seals haul out on to ice or land for this process.

All species have a single pup per year, and females mate again shortly after giving birth. The newly fertilised egg doesn't immediately begin developing, but hangs in a state of suspended animation for a few months before it implants in the uterine wall and begins to grow. In this way, the females do not have the added stress of nursing one pup while growing another one, and the pups are born only in the spring or summer when conditions are the least harsh.

mammals

Weddell seal and pup

Even so, consider the dramatic change of environment experienced by a Weddell seal when it is born: it goes from being inside its mother, where conditions are sheltered and a warm 37°C (99°F), to lying on the ice at possibly -40°C (-40°F), with a strong wind blowing. And the pup is wet! One of the things that helps a pup survive this huge change of circumstances is that it immediately begins to gorge itself on milk, gaining more than 2 kg (4.4 lb) a day. The milk is very rich, with a fat content of as much as 40 percent. By comparison, the average cow's milk consumed by humans is about 4 percent fat.

Unlike Antarctic birds, the males do not make any contribution to rearing the pups, and most are not even present during the nursing stages. Leopard, Ross and crabeater seals all breed as isolated individuals; Weddell seals form clusters of breeding females. Southern elephant seals and Antarctic fur seals, the land-breeders, reproduce in dense colonies, with the males fighting for control of, and access to, females. But once the pups are born the males take no responsibility for their care.

IDENTIFICATION

The identification of Antarctic seals is relatively straightforward. The Antarctic fur seal is unmistakable, as it is the only seal here that can sit upright on its front flippers, just like the performing sea lions in circuses and oceanaria. All the other Antarctic seals have only short flippers and move on land by inching along, rather in the manner of a giant slug. Body size and colouration are the main features used to identify the phocid seals.

Phocid seals

All the seals you will see in Antarctica, with the sole exception of the Antarctic fur seal, belong to the family *Phocidae*. These seals – the crabeater, leopard, Ross, Weddell and southern elephant – are earless – that is, they have no external ear flap, just a small surface opening to the auditory canal at the back of their head. Their forelimbs are highly reduced in size, and used only to aid steering underwater and to have the odd scratch on land. An exception to this rule is the leopard seal, which uses its very long front flippers for swimming, flapping them to great effect and achieving fast speeds. A thick layer of blubber (rather than fur) insulates these seals from the cold.

Eared seals

The Antarctic fur seal is an *Otariid*, or eared seal, with a conspicuous external ear located behind the eye. As their name suggests, Antarctic fur seals have a rich coat of fur covering their body and because of this they were the favourites of sealers in the 1800s. Their fur consists of two type of hair: an outer guard hair which is stout and wiry and, beneath this, fibres that are fine and softer and which provide insulation and warmth. They do not have a blubber layer. Fur seals use their large forelimbs to provide thrust during swimming. They are also unique among Antarctic seals in that they can rotate their hind flippers forward and support some of their body weight on these limbs. This makes them very agile and fast when moving on shore.

mammals

SCIENTIFIC NAME
Arctocephalus gazella

POPULATION SIZE
c. 3 million

DISTRIBUTION
islands south of the Antarctic Convergence, South Georgia (about 95% of world population breeds there), South Shetlands, South Orkneys, some Indian Ocean islands and Macquarie Island

CONSERVATION STATUS
least concern

BODY SIZE
length
**males – up to 1.9 m (6 ft)
females – up to 1.3 m (4.3 ft)**
weight
**males – *c.* 170 kg (374 lb)
females – *c.* 40 kg (88 lb)**

DIET
krill, fish, squid

DIVING BEHAVIOUR
maximum depth
181 m (593 ft)

maximum duration
10 minutes

BREEDING
pups born late November or early December
age at weaning
16 weeks

Antarctic fur seals are the only seal species in the region that can stand on all four limbs. While all the other species move on land and ice like blubbery inchworms, leaving a furrow-like trail behind them, fur seals are capable of rotating their hind flippers forward to raise themselves off the ground. They can also run faster than most people, especially those wearing a parka and rubber boots, so care is needed when visiting fur seal beaches.

Male fur seals are very aggressive during the breeding season (November to mid January) and defend their territories with vigour against encroaching male seals or humans of either sex. They maintain these territories in order to have exclusive breeding access to the females that settle in them; males that do not hold territories seldom mate. However, holding on to a territory is difficult, with only the largest and best fighters managing the task. Territory-holders must fast for most of the two months or so they hold a territory, since going to sea to feed leaves a vacancy that is quickly filled. Most pups are born in early December and do not finish nursing until April.

Fur seal numbers in the Antarctic Peninsula region increase towards the end of summer as male seals leave the huge breeding grounds in South Georgia and move south to feed. Because the females are suckling pups on the breeding grounds until autumn, any fur seals seen around the peninsula will almost certainly be males. Outside of the breeding season, males are surprisingly skittish and a minimum approach distance of 15 m (50 ft) is recommended.

The population of Antarctic fur seals has recovered remarkably since their near-extinction from commercial harvesting in the early 1800s. As recently as 1933, it was estimated that there were only 60 living on Bird Island in South Georgia. Today, the population there exceeds 65,000.

mammals

Crabeater seal

SCIENTIFIC NAME
Lobodon carcinophagus

POPULATION SIZE
10 million+

DISTRIBUTION
**circumpolar; confined
to the pack-ice zone
of Antarctica**

CONSERVATION STATUS
least concern

BODY SIZE
length
up to 2.4 m (8 ft)
weight
c. **225 kg (495 lb)
females are slightly
larger than males**

LIFESPAN
**up to 40 years, but
25 is more typical**

DIET
krill

DIVING BEHAVIOUR
**usually less than
30 m (98 ft)**
maximum depth
430 m (1411 ft)
maximum duration
11 minutes

BREEDING
**pups born September
and October**
age at weaning
3 weeks

Crabeater seals don't really eat crabs, they eat krill, and no other seal is so specialised for consuming just one type of food. Where most mammals have molars for chewing or cutting food, crabeater seals have molars that are highly modified for filtering food from water. Each tooth has at least four lobes, and when the mouth is closed the upper and lower teeth mesh to form a sieve that traps krill while water is expelled (see page 227).

Crabeater seals are probably the most common seal in the world, yet few people see them because they inhabit the pack-ice zone around Antarctica. In the ice, they are often found in groups ranging from a few animals to herds of hundreds. They seldom haul out on land.

The unstable nature of the pack-ice habitat may at least partially explain the short, three-week nursing period of this seal. In such a changeable environment as drifting ice, a pup that gets separated from its mother will likely starve. Being dependent on mum for only a short time is, therefore, advantageous to survival.

During the spring breeding season, female crabeaters and their pups are scattered widely, and often attended by a male who will attempt to mate with the female when she becomes sexually receptive after her pup is weaned. Before this, males attempt to mate but are rebuffed by the larger females, and these encounters often leave the ice floe splattered with the male's blood. The male will also combat any other males that try to encroach on his floe and female.

Leopard seals and killer whales prey on crabeater seals, particularly young seals in their first year. Many who escape these predators wear the scars of the attacks on their fur.

SCIENTIFIC NAME
Hydrurga leptonyx

POPULATION SIZE
220,000+

DISTRIBUTION
**circumpolar, rare
outside of Antarctica**

CONSERVATION STATUS
least concern

BODY SIZE
length
**male – up to 3 m
(10.9 ft)
female – up to 3.8 m
(12.5 ft)**
weight
male – *c.* **300 kg
(660 lb)
female –** *c.* **500 kg
(1100 lb)**

DIET
**krill, seals, penguins,
fish**

DIVING BEHAVIOUR
not known

BREEDING
**pups probably born
October to mid November**
age at weaning
c. **4 weeks**

Leopard seals are well-known for eating penguins, especially newly fledged chicks, but krill makes up a far larger component of their diet. The seals' molars are highly modified for filtering these small crustaceans from the water. Each tooth has three cusps. When the mouth is closed, the teeth from the upper and lower jaws fit together to form an effective sieve.

However, the leopard seal's reputation as a top predator of warm-blooded prey is deserved, with crabeater seal pups and young penguins being particularly important in their summer diet. Leopard seals prefer to eat the blubber of these animals, which they skin by thrashing the body back and forth on the surface. They then scrape the fat off the now inside-out skin and usually leave the rest of the carcass to scavenging birds such as skuas and giant petrels. Their penguin-hunting behaviour is most common late in the summer, when the chicks take their first foraging trips in the water.

Leopard seals have attacked humans on several occasions. In most cases, the person attacked was walking on sea ice when the seal lunged out of the water at them. It's possible the seal mistook their vertical profile for that of an emperor penguin, a common prey species. The only documented human fatality from leopard seal attack occurred in July 2003, when a British scientist was killed while snorkelling as part of a research programme near Rothera Research Station. With an increasing number of recreational scuba divers visiting Antarctica, the number of aggressive encounters with these animals may increase.

Leopard seals are not gregarious and spend most of their time in the pack-ice zone. Little is known about their reproductive behaviour. Juvenile animals sometimes wander well north of Antarctica, turning up in South America, New Zealand and Australia.

mammals

ABOVE *Smaller Antarctic fur seals mix with southern elephant seals on a beach*
BELOW LEFT *Moulting southern elephant seal, huddled with others for warmth*

Southern elephant seal

SCIENTIFIC NAME
Mirounga leonina

POPULATION SIZE
c. 640,000

DISTRIBUTION
**breeds on subantarctic
islands and Antarctic
Peninsula and adjacent
islands**

CONSERVATION STATUS
**least concern;
south Atlantic population
stable; south Pacific
and south Indian Ocean
populations declining**

BODY SIZE
length
**male – up to 5 m
(16.5 ft)
female – up to 3 m
(10 ft)**
weight
**male – c. 3700 kg
(8140 lb)
female – c. 800 kg
(1760 lb)**

DIET
deep-sea fish, squid

DIVING BEHAVIOUR
maximum depth
1631 m (5351 ft)
maximum duration
120 minutes

BREEDING
pups born October
age at weaning
24 days

The southern elephant seal is superlative in several ways. It is the largest of all seals: the males can weigh more than two rhinoceroses or two hippopotamuses. It is also the most accomplished diver, and has been recorded descending more than 1.6 km (1 mile) underwater. Females tend to dive deeper than males, although males' dives are often of greater duration.

Elephant seals need to come ashore only to breed and to moult, and more than 80 percent of their time is spent in the ocean. Breeding takes place in the spring, when males fight among themselves for control of groups of females. Subordinate males are aggressively chased off, but if they choose to stay and fight, the violent combat sees the loser sent on his way with many bloody wounds about the face and neck. Males can be as much as 10 times larger than females. A dominant male, sometimes called a beachmaster, will mate with all the females within the group he controls. This takes place a few weeks after the pups are born, while the females are still in attendance on shore. Females nurse their pups for about three and a half weeks, and fast throughout this time.

From the time of their discovery, elephant seals were exploited for the fine oil that could be rendered from their blubber. Over-harvesting led to their extinction as a commercial species in the 1800s, but by 1910 their numbers had increased sufficiently for further hunting to begin. The last commercial hunt for elephant seals took place in 1964 in South Georgia. Since then these animals have been protected. The population in the South Atlantic is now stable or increasing slightly, while in the southern Indian and Pacific Oceans it is declining for reasons that are not fully understood. Changes in availability of prey may be a factor, as increased sea temperatures have reduced biological productivity in some areas.

mammals

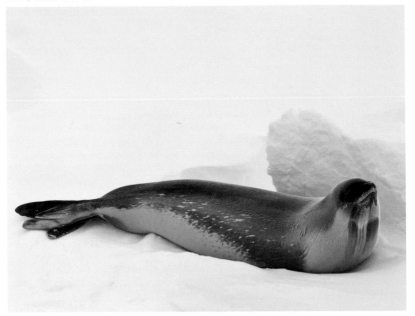

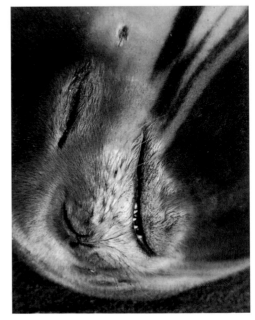

SCIENTIFIC NAME
Ommatophoca rossi

POPULATION SIZE
**20,000+; possibly as
high as 220,000**

DISTRIBUTION
**circumpolar; confined
to Antarctica, especially
zone of heavy pack ice**

CONSERVATION STATUS
least concern

BODY SIZE
length
**male – up to 2 m
(6.5 ft)
female – up to 2.5 m
(8.3 ft)**
weight
**both sexes – *c*. 200 kg
(440 lb)**

DIET
**large squid, fish, small
amounts of krill**

DIVING BEHAVIOUR
maximum depth
212 m (696 ft)
maximum duration
10 minutes

BREEDING
**pups probably born
in November**
age at weaning
***c*. 4 weeks**

Because the Ross seal resides in the areas of Antarctic seas where the pack ice is densest, it is perhaps not surprising that much about its biology remains unknown: these areas are so difficult for biologists to reach that the little information we have has been gleaned during rushed visits or lucky sightings.

Ross seals are the shortest of the Antarctic seals, with very small heads and tiny teeth. Their eyes, however, are extremely large, and are thought to be an adaptation for feeding on squid in the low-light conditions found at depth under the pack ice.

It appears that the Ross seals take much larger species of squid than other seals. This, combined with their tendency to inhabit the densest ice areas, probably reduces feeding competition with the other seal species. It may also protect them from such predators as killer whales, which are restricted to areas of looser ice where they feed on other seals.

When out of the water, Ross seals seem to be more vocal than other Antarctic seals. A variety of calls, trills and pulsed chugs have been reported.

Ross seals have never been commercially harvested, and because of their relatively small population they are fully protected under the Antarctic Treaty System.

mammals

Weddell seal

SCIENTIFIC NAME
Leptonychotes weddelli

POPULATION SIZE
500,000+

DISTRIBUTION
**circumpolar, confined
to Antarctica, although
small populations on
South Georgia and
Bouvetøya**

CONSERVATION STATUS
least concern

BODY SIZE
length
**male – up to 2.9 m
(9.5 ft)
female – up to 3.3 m
(10.9 ft)**
weight
**both sexes – c. 400 kg
(880 lb)**

DIET
fish, squid

DIVING BEHAVIOUR
maximum depth
750 m (2461 ft)
maximum duration
73 minutes

BREEDING
**pups born late
September to
early November**
age at weaning
7 weeks

The southernmost mammal in the world, the
Weddell seal is the only species that inhabits the
fast-ice zone fringing the Antarctic continent.
In this zone the sea freezes in solid sheets that
fasten on to the land, forming an almost uniform
roof over the water. For air-breathing, fish-eating
animals such as seals, this ice forms a major obstacle
when foraging or breathing. Weddell seals manage to
survive here because of their prodigious diving ability –
they can stay submerged for more than an hour – and
because they maintain holes in the ice by using their
unusually protruding incisors to scrape an opening.
This activity is hard on teeth. Many older Weddell seals
die by drowning when their teeth become so worn
they are unable to keep a hole open.

Weddell seals mate in the water after the pups are
weaned. Males fight among themselves for access to
females by patrolling underwater territories and
controlling the access to breathing holes. The diving
behaviour of Weddell seals has been studied in
more detail than that of most Antarctic species, and
their abilities underwater are remarkable. In addition
to the great depths and duration of dives, they also
have a short recovery time between dives and make
many foraging trips without the need to rest long on
the surface.

You are more likely to see Weddell seals hauled out
on land or snow patches than on ice floes.

mammals

Humpback whale, Paradise Harbour

Whales

Spotting whales in the icy waters of the Southern Ocean is often regarded as one of the highlights of a cruise to Antarctica. Provided you spend time on deck and keep your eyes focused for the tell-tale signs of a waterspout, dorsal fin or tail fluke, you will be rewarded with a glimpse of some of the most remarkable animals on Earth. Calm seas and dull, flat light are the best conditions for spotting whales. Unlike in most regions of the world, if you see a dorsal fin you can guarantee that it belongs to a whale, as there are no sharks in Antarctica.

The whales, including the dolphins and porpoises, are also known as cetaceans, belonging to the group *Cetacea*. The name comes from the Greek *ketos*, meaning 'large sea creature'. Whales are mammals, not fish. They breathe air using lungs, give birth to live young, produce milk from mammary glands to feed their calves, and maintain a constant core body temperature of around 37°C (98°F).

Worldwide there are 85 species of cetacean, which can be broadly divided into baleen whales (15 species) and toothed whales (70 species). The Southern Ocean is richly populated with whales, with more than 10 species commonly found inhabiting the waters near the continent. Whales are most likely to be seen during the summer months from January to March, when they migrate south to take advantage of the abundant food on offer. The timing is perfect, as this activity coincides with the peak in Antarctic cruise operations.

mammals

Antarctic whales
- Arnoux's beaked
- Blue
- Fin
- Killer
- Antarctic minke
- Humpback
- Sei
- Southern bottlenose
- Southern right
- Sperm
- Hourglass dolphin

Whale facts
- mammals (not fish)
- evolved from land mammals
- give birth to live young
- produce milk to feed young
- are warm-blooded (endothermic)
- have hair (although only a few 'whiskers')
- breathe air through blow-holes (nostrils)
- are carnivorous predators
- forelimbs are flippers
- hindlimbs have disappeared (only the pelvis remains floating in the body)
- the tail (flukes) moves up and down, not side to side as in fish

BODY FORM

Whales evolved from land mammals that invaded the aquatic environment more than 50 million years ago. Today they spend their lives entirely in water and have features which typify an aquatic existence. Their bodies are torpedo-shaped (fusiform), with no obvious neck or shoulders; this streamlining reduces drag as they swim through the water.

They have no external ears, the forelimbs are modified into paddles or flippers for steering, and all that remains of the hindlimbs are remnants of the pelvic girdle, comprising two small bones which are suspended loosely in the body wall. Male genitalia are internalised and the penis is retractable.

The tail is modified into flukes (two lobes), which move up and down to provide thrust. In contrast, a fish's tail moves from side to side.

The nostrils of whales have moved during evolution to the top of the head to form blow-holes. The blow-holes allow ventilation of the lungs, often in spectacular fashion. The lungs and ribcage are highly elastic, and because of a diagonally positioned diaphragm whales are

*All toothed whales such as the killer whale (top) have one nostril, or blow-hole;
all baleen whales have two, as shown by the minke whale (above left);*
ABOVE RIGHT *Blue whale, exhaling.*

able to empty 90 percent of the air in their lungs when exhaling. This
forced exhalation results in the whale's 'blow' or 'waterspout'. The
spout is caused by the warm air in the lungs condensing as it hits the
cooler atmosphere, and surplus water lying over the blow-hole being
ejected upwards. The size, shape and angle of the blow are unique to
each species.

A resounding feature of many whales, especially those species present in Antarctic waters, is their massive size. The blue whale, the world's largest living animal, can grow in excess of 30 m (100 ft) long. It is 100 million times heavier than the world's smallest mammal, the Kitti's hog-nosed bat.

This large body size is an advantage in the icy waters, as the surface area of the animal relative to its volume is greatly reduced, retarding heat loss. A thick layer of blubber, composed of fats and oils, also provides insulation, as well as aiding the whale's buoyancy and acting as an important energy fuel-store. The blubber can represent more than 30 percent of the body weight of the whale. It is not unusual for some whale species to rely entirely on blubber stores for 6 to 8 months, as they fast while travelling to and from their breeding grounds.

Blue whale

BEHAVIOUR

Humpback whale

Whales spend most of their lives underwater, holding their breath; they need to return to the surface only to replenish their oxygen stores. Some whales have been recorded diving for more than an hour. The sperm whale is the deep-diving champion. There are records of sperm whales descending more than 3100 m (10,230 ft) to hunt down prey such as deep-sea giant squid.

These incredible feats are achieved in part by the whale storing large quantities of oxygen in the blood and muscle, binding it with haemoglobin and myoglobin, respectively. Surprisingly, the lungs are not a major provider of oxygen during dives, with some whales even exhaling before diving.

All whales are carnivorous predators. While some eat small planktonic animals by filter-feeding, others actively chase down fish and squid and, in case of the killer whale, the occasional penguin, seal or even large whale.

Many whales undertake seasonal migrations between breeding grounds and feeding grounds. This is especially true of Antarctic whales, although there is gathering evidence to suggest that some species may be resident year-round in the unfrozen regions of the Southern Ocean. Others migrate northwards to lower latitudes and warmer waters to mate and give birth to their young.

mammals

IDENTIFICATION

Identifying whales is challenging, as you will often get only glimpses of the animals as they come to the surface to breathe. However, some species – such as the killer whale with its black and white patterning, and the adult male's large triangular dorsal fin – are unmistakable.

Distinguishing one whale species from another relies on looking at the blow, the shape and position of the dorsal fin, the shape of the tail flukes, the body colouration, and the behavioural characteristics, such as raising the tail during a dive, putting the head out of the water (spyhopping), and leaping completely out of the water (breaching).

Toothed whales

Eighty percent of all cetaceans, including the dolphins and porpoises, are toothed whales. These range in size from the sperm whale at 18 m (60 ft) to some of the dolphins at less than 1.5 m (5 ft). Many have peg-like teeth, although there are many exceptions to this rule.

Located in the forehead of toothed whales is a round, lens-shaped, oil-filled structure known as the melon. The melon is thought to be used in echo-location by focusing the sounds generated in the nasal passages and then projecting them forwards. The returning sounds are then picked up by the lower jaw and transmitted to the inner ear. The time it takes for the sounds to return, and the changes that occur to them en route, are used by the whale to locate prey and to navigate – a method that is not unlike sonar.

Toothed whale facts
- also known as the *Odontocete* ('toothed whales')
- includes the dolphins & porpoises
- largest is the sperm whale
- have a single blow-hole
- feed on squid & fish
- asymmetrical skull
- use echo-location

Baleen whales

Less than 20 percent of cetaceans are baleen whales, and these differ from toothed whales in several ways. Principally, they lack teeth and instead have plates of baleen hanging inside the mouth from the upper jaw (see photograph). Baleen is made of keratin, the same as our fingernails, and the plates filter small plankton and fish from water.

Right whales were some of the earliest whales to be hunted and killed. These were the 'right' whales to capture, as they were slow-moving, travelled close to coastlines, and, because of their high oil content, floated when dead. Right whales can be easily identified by the white patches, or callosities, around their heads. These raised areas of skin are often covered in encrusting barnacles. Right whales have very large baleen plates, and feed by continuously straining zooplankton as they swim along. The species is now extremely rare in Antarctic waters.

The groove-throated whales include the blue, fin, sei, minke and humpback. The grooves, or pleats, in the bottom jaw of these whales are expandable and allow large mouthfuls of sea water to be taken. Contraction of the throat grooves, together with upward movement of the tongue, squeezes the sea water across the baleen plates, catching food on the inside and spilling water out over the lips.

mammals

Baleen whale facts
- known also as the *Mysticete* ('moustached whales')
- includes the rorquals, right whales & grey whales
- largest is the blue whale
- have two blow-holes
- filter feeders on plankton & small fish
- enormous head, 20 percent of body length

SCIENTIFIC NAME
Balaenoptera musculus

POPULATION SIZE
5000–10,000 in southern hemisphere

DISTRIBUTION
worldwide

CONSERVATION STATUS
endangered

BODY SIZE
length
up to 33.5 m (110 ft)
weight
150,000 kg (165 tons); females are slightly larger than males

LIFESPAN
80 years

DIET
krill

DIVING BEHAVIOUR
typically short dives (average 7 minutes' duration). Over 100 m (330 ft) deep
maximum depth
500 m (1640 ft)
maximum duration
30 minutes

BREEDING
sexual maturity at 6–10 years breed every 2–3 years
gestation
1 year
age at weaning
7–8 months

The blue whale is the largest living animal on Earth. Reaching a length of 30 m (100 ft), it is probably the largest species ever to have existed – larger even than the dinosaurs. Females tend to grow slightly bigger than the males, and calves are born at a huge 7 m (25 ft) long and around 3000 kg (3.3 tons) in weight.

Blue whales are exceptional filter-feeders, targeting the rich supply of krill in the Southern Ocean in the summer months and consuming over 3000 to 5000 kg (3 to 5 tons) of food daily. They use a stack of 300 to 400 baleen plates and their expandable mouth to filter the krill from large gulps of sea water.

Low-frequency calls allow blue whales to communicate with each other over hundreds, if not thousands, of kilometres of ocean.

Consider yourself extremely privileged if you get to see one of these remarkable animals. Hunted almost to extinction in the twentieth century, when over 350,000 were killed, the blue whale is making only a slow recovery and is still considered endangered. Little is known about their lives, owing to their secretive nature and the difficulty of locating them. They tend to be found in pods of only two or three animals, although if the feeding is good congregations of more than 30 have been observed.

Key points to look out for when spotting a blue whale are its large body size and its pale turquoise-blue-grey colour. The dorsal fin is very small in relation to the body and occurs well back on the spine, towards the tail flukes. Also look out for the size of its blow or waterspout, which can extend 9 m (30 ft) into the air.

mammals

Fin whale

SCIENTIFIC NAME
Balaenoptera physalus

POPULATION SIZE
15,000–20,000 in southern hemisphere

DISTRIBUTION
worldwide

CONSERVATION STATUS
endangered

BODY SIZE
length
up to 27 m (88 ft)
weight
up to 80,000 kg (88 tons); females are larger than males

LIFESPAN
85–90 years

DIET
krill

DIVING BEHAVIOUR
typically short dives (5–8 min), up to 100 m (330 ft) deep
maximum depth
560 m (1840 ft)
maximum duration
17–20 min

BREEDING
sexual maturity at 7–9 years
breed every 2–3 years
gestation
11 months
age at weaning
6–8 months

The fin whale is the world's second largest animal after the blue whale, and grows to a length of 27 m (88 feet). It is also one of the fastest whales and can sustain speeds in excess of 35 kph (21 mph).

Despite their great size, fin whales are less conspicuous than many other species as they seldom jump and splash about, and do not show their tail flukes when commencing a dive. Identification can be difficult. Look for their broad, flat head with its prominent splashguard in front of the blow-hole. The spout, or blow, is very tall and narrow and on windless days will reach a height of 8 m (26 feet).

Fin whales have asymmetrical colouring. The jaw and frontmost baleen plates on the right side are white, while on the left side they are a darker grey. The whales use the pale side to startle their prey, krill, and herd it into a tight mass. They then open their huge mouths and engulf the ball of krill – along with lots of water. An adult fin whale takes only three seconds to fill its mouth with up to 68,000 litres (17,969 gallons) of sea water.

Fin whales breed in temperate and tropical waters, migrating to the Southern Ocean each summer to feed on the abundant krill. Commercial whalers originally ignored fin whales as they were too fast to catch. Modern ships changed that, and between 1905 and 1976 over 700,000 fin whales were killed in the southern hemisphere. Despite a moratorium on hunting fin whales since 1986, they are still listed as endangered. Between 2005 and 2007, a Japanese fleet killed 20 fin whales in the Antarctic as part of a scientific programme, and the government has declared plans to increase this figure to 50 per year.

SCIENTIFIC NAME
Megaptera novaeangliae

POPULATION SIZE
30,000–40,000 globally

DISTRIBUTION
worldwide

CONSERVATION STATUS
least concern

BODY SIZE
length
males – up to 16 m (52 ft)
females – up to 17 m (56 ft)
weight
males – 33,000 kg
(32.5 tons)
females – 36,000 kg
(35.4 tons)

LIFESPAN
70–80 years

DIET
krill, zooplankton,
small fish

DIVING BEHAVIOUR
maximum depth
176 m (577 ft)
maximum duration
25 minutes

BREEDING
in northerly warmer,
tropical waters
sexual maturity at
6–10 years
breed every 2–3 years
(usually single calf)
gestation
12 months
age at weaning
1 year

The slow-moving humpback whale is the most conspicuous of the Antarctic whales, often seen swimming on the surface or splashing about while feeding. If this isn't enough to make them a crowd favourite, some animals also have a tendency to approach ships. Unlike the many whale species that show only a small portion of their back at the surface, humpbacks frequently spyhop, or slap the surface of the water with their extremely long front flippers. Other attention-grabbing antics include slapping the water with their tail (lobtailing) and breaching.

At the start of a deep dive, humpbacks arch their backs and stick their tail vertically in the air. This reveals the black and white pattern on the underside – which is unique to each individual and useful for identification.

The humpbacks seen in the waters around the Antarctic Peninsula are summer visitors only, having migrated from their calving grounds off Brazil. Although mating and calving take place in the warmer waters of the tropics to subtropics, the whales seldom feed in these areas. Instead, they migrate to take advantage of the excellent feeding conditions in the cold productive seas around Antarctica. Their staple diet is krill, which they filter from the water using the bristles of the 600 or so baleen plates that hang from the roof of their mouth.

Male humpback whales produce complex songs associated with mating. These are the longest vocalisations in the animal world and vary among populations. The local song also changes over several seasons, and all the males in the population somehow stay current with the changes. A humpback song usually lasts 10 to 15 minutes, although they sometimes go on for 30 minutes before being repeated. Their exact function is unknown, although they are most frequently produced on the breeding grounds, and only by males.

mammals

SCIENTIFIC NAME
Orcinus orca

POPULATION SIZE
50,000+ in Southern Ocean

DISTRIBUTION
**worldwide, circumpolar
in southern hemisphere**

CONSERVATION STATUS
**lower risk, conservation-
dependent**

BODY SIZE
length
**males – up to 10 m (33 ft)
females – up to 8.5 m (28 ft)**
weight
**males – 11,000 kg (11 tons)
females – 7,500 kg (7 tons)**

LIFESPAN
**50–80 years (females
tend to live longer)**

DIET
**fish, squid, penguins,
seals and occasionally
baleen whales**

DIVING BEHAVIOUR
**short dives, typically
less than 5 minutes**

BREEDING
**sexual maturity at
10–18 years
breed every 3–8 years**
gestation
14–17 months
age at weaning
1 year

The killer whale is the largest member of the dolphin family. It has prominent black and white markings and a large conical head, making it the most recognisable of all whale species. Mature males have a characteristic triangular dorsal fin that can reach 1.8 m (6 ft) in height, whereas immature males and females have small, slightly curved dorsal fins.

The white eye-patch and the underside of killer whales in Antarctic waters often take on a yellow colouration from staining by small yellow-brown phytoplankton (algae).

Killer whales have the longest gestation period of all cetaceans, lasting up to 17 months. Females bear a single calf every 3 to 8 years. The social structure of killer-whale pods appears highly complex and variable. Some groups appear to have a matriarchal structure, with the offspring staying with the mother for life, while others have individuals that come and go. They are usually found in pods of 5 to 10 in the Southern Ocean.

Killer whales are so called because they feed on large marine mammals, such as seals and the occasional baleen whale. They hunt down their prey cooperatively, and you will often see them hanging around penguin and seal colonies. There have been no reports of killer whales killing humans in the wild.

mammals

SCIENTIFIC NAME
Balaenoptera bonaerensis

POPULATION SIZE
400,000–1,000,000 in southern hemisphere

DISTRIBUTION
circumpolar in southern hemisphere (separate northern hemisphere species)

CONSERVATION STATUS
lower risk, conservation-dependent

BODY SIZE
length
up to 10.5 m (35 ft)
weight
8600 kg (9.5 tons)
Females tend to be slightly larger than males

LIFESPAN
50–60 years

DIET
krill, small fish

DIVING BEHAVIOUR
typically short, shallow dives, 3–8 minutes in duration.

BREEDING
sexual maturity at 5–8 years breed every 2–3 years; but some populations may breed annually.
calves born May–August
gestation
10 months
age at weaning
12 months

The minke is the smallest baleen whale in Antarctic waters, and is found in open water as well as among pack ice. Minkes have a slender, torpedo-shaped body with a sharply pointed head, and grow to a body length of around 10 m (33 ft). As with most rorqual-baleen whales – that is, those with throat pleats – the females grow slightly larger than the males.

Minke whales are the most abundant of all baleen whales and there is some evidence that they may reproduce more frequently than others, possibly on an annual cycle.

Minkes are reasonably easy is to identify. Often occurring in groups of 3 to 10, they tend to be fast-moving, have a sharp, prominent dorsal fin and, when viewed from a large cruise ship, look almost like large dolphins swimming through the water. They do not show their tail flukes when diving.

In pack ice, minkes will sometimes 'spyhop' (as pictured left) to seek alternative breathing sites.

Minke whales are classified by the IUCN as 'lower risk – conservation-dependent'. Despite this, for the past decade in Antarctic waters they have been the target of Japanese whaling operations, with the 2006 annual quota being set at more than 900 animals.

mammals

Threats to Antarctic conservation

THE ANTARCTIC TREATY

The Antarctic Treaty plays a key role in protecting Antarctica and its wildlife.
The adoption of the Madrid Environmental Protocol regulating human activity,
the 50-year moratorium on mining, and the setting up of environmental
monitoring bodies such as the Commission for the Conservation of Antarctic
Marine Living Resources (CCAMLR) are all designed to ensure that Antarctica
is conserved well into the future. Unfortunately, however, while these regulations
cover the monitoring of Antarctic activities, they provide no means of policing
what is done in the region.

The Antarctic Treaty was signed in Washington, D.C. on December 1, 1959 by 12
states, and entered into force for those states on June 23, 1961. As of April 2011,
48 countries had acceded to the Treaty.

ORIGINAL SIGNATORIES, 1959
United Kingdom, South Africa, Belgium, Japan, United States of America, Norway,
France, New Zealand, Russia (then Soviet Union), Argentina, Australia, Chile

1961 Poland	1983 People's Republic of China India	1990 Switzerland
1965 Denmark		1991 Guatemala
1967 Netherlands	1984 Hungary Sweden Finland Cuba	1992 Ukraine
1971 Romania		1993 Czech Republic Slovak Republic
1974 Germany	1986 Republic of Korea	1996 Turkey
1975 Papua New Guinea Brazil	1987 Greece Democratic People's Republic of Korea Austria Ecuador	1999 Venezuela
1978 Bulgaria		2001 Estonia
1980 Uruguay	1988 Canada	2006 Belarus
1981 Italy Peru Spain	1989 Colombia	2008 Monaco 2010 Portugal

CONSERVATION

Antarctica is a fragile ecosystem, intricately linked to the rest of the planet. It is regarded as the most pristine place on Earth and for many people it takes on a sanctuary status. However, what is not always realised is that Antarctica and its wildlife are vulnerable to human activities elsewhere. Environmental disturbances that occur in the northern hemisphere can sometimes be felt in the deep south. And Antarctic organisms are so highly specialised that even small changes in environmental conditions can have disastrous consequences, changing forever the structure of the ecosystem.

The threats Antarctica faces in the near future are all a consequence of human activity. Sealing, whaling and fishing have taken their toll on the ecosystem, and continue to do so. More importantly, the threat of global warming and subsequent climate change is hanging over the continent, indicating more than ever that our past activities are catching up with us. Antarctica is in the front line.

More than a third of the wildlife described in this book is listed on the IUCN Red List of Threatened Species (see page 273). Even as you cruise across the Southern Ocean on your way to Antarctica, it is worth remembering that the albatrosses and giant petrels following your ship are suffering serious population declines. For most people it takes just one day in Antarctica to realise what we will lose if we don't act to protect this environment against exploitation and habitat destruction. This is a good thing: the more people who become aware, the greater the chance of protecting what is left. We hope the magic of experiencing Antarctica and seeing its wildlife will have this effect on you.

SEALING

The start of human-induced environmental change in Antarctica began with the exploitation of the continent's unique resources. The sealers in the 1800s were the first to recognise the existence of bountiful natural resources in the waters south of Cape Horn, and they hunted down vast numbers of Antarctic fur seals for their warm and luxurious pelts. The mass slaughter was short-lived, as populations were decimated and financial returns from travelling south became unprofitable within only a few decades. The threat of extinction of some populations initiated a protection status for fur seals and a ban on hunting in South Georgia, where the population is centred. As a part of the United Kingdom, this protected status pre-dates the Antarctic Treaty. As a result of this intervention, the seal populations have now recovered and returned to pre-hunting levels.

Antarctic fur seal

WHALING

The exploitation of whales in Antarctica is undoubtedly one of the darkest episodes in the continent's history. During the first half of the twentieth century, large baleen whales were killed for their blubber, meat, oil and bone. Several species, such as blue whales and fin whales, were hunted to the brink of extinction.

Whaling operations began in Antarctic waters in 1905. South Georgia was the centre of activity, with blue, fin and sei whales being targeted. Steam-powered boats and explosive harpoons, developed in the late 1860s, were highly effective.

The introduction of floating factory ships in the 1920s accelerated the exploitation. Such ships could travel further south, allowing whales to be processed on board, rather than transported to land for dismemberment. Hundreds of thousands of whales were taken from the Southern Ocean, resulting in serious population declines.

In 1946 the International Whaling Commission (IWC) was set up to regulate whaling activity, and in 1965 the blue whale was the first species to be given protection. In 1986, the IWC introduced a moratorium on all commercial whaling worldwide.

Whaling is now back on the agenda. Since the mid 1980s, Japanese whalers have been hunting and killing minke whales in the Southern Ocean as part of a scientific study to assess the feasibility of a sustainable harvest. In 2006, they increased their quota from 440 to 935 whales, and included the humpback and fin whales as part of their future diet. The moratorium on all commercial whaling is hotly debated within the IWC, with Japan actively lobbying small nations for their vote to restart commercial hunting.

A highlight of any cruise to Antarctica is the sight of great baleen whales. All are listed on the IUCN Red List of Threatened Species, yet the pressure is on to hunt them for commercial gain. If there were ever a case for making Antarctica a wildlife sanctuary it would be to protect these remarkable animals.

threats to Antarctica

FISHING

Commercial fishing in Antarctica began in the 1960s, with both fish and krill being targeted. There was a boom in krill fishing in the 1970s, but this soon faded because of problems experienced with krill decomposing during storage and transportation. Recently, however, there has been a new increase in fin-fishing operations and these are now posing a serious threat, not only to the stability of fish stocks but also because of the associated indiscriminate killing of sea birds.

Most of the fishing in the Southern Ocean is by longlining, which involves trailing baited hooks and lines behind a fishing vessel. Some lines are more than 100 km (62 miles) long and have tens of thousands of baited hooks. Longlines are extremely effective in capturing large fish. Unfortunately, sea birds are also captured: in attempting to take the bait while on the surface, they get caught, become entangled, and eventually get pulled under and drown.

More than 100,000 birds are killed this way each year, especially albatrosses, giant petrels and white-chinned petrels. CCAMLR has been closely monitoring this bycatch and regulating fishing practices. Measures to reduce the number of sea-bird deaths include the use of water sprays while lines are being fed out, faster-sinking lines, and setting lines at night. However, illegal fishing operations are problematic as the owners do not employ recommended methods.

In the 1980s, the mackerel icefish was targeted by the fishing operations, but these days the Patagonian and Antarctic toothfish (also known as Antarctic cod) are the prized catches. Toothfish are large (2 m/6.5 ft) mid- to deep-water species (400 m/1300 ft). They are slow-growing, reach sexual maturity between 10 and 12 years, and have a white, creamy flesh that is highly sought after.

The Antarctic toothfish is found below the Antarctic Convergence, and the Patagonian toothfish in the more northerly, warmer waters. There is a considerable black market for these fish, which are often disguised by being called Chilean sea bass, especially in the lucrative US market. Illegal operations targeting Patagonian toothfish have decimated stocks over the past decade; now attention is turning to the more southerly Antarctic toothfish.

INVASION OF ALIEN SPECIES

In recent years, a new threat has begun to take hold. Non-native microbes, plants and animals are appearing and establishing themselves on land and in the waters surrounding Antarctica. The arrival of alien species represents a serious threat as they are likely to upset the delicate balance of the Antarctic ecosystem, competing with and displacing native species and so changing the continent's biodiversity.

As the northernmost part of Antarctica, the peninsula is particularly vulnerable. Blue-green algae have recently arrived at King George Island, and the North Atlantic spider crab (*Hyas araneus*) has been found in waters near the peninsula. It appears these outsiders may have hitched a ride on ships travelling to Antarctica, unbeknown to the scientists or tourists on board. Water in ships' ballast tanks can transport organisms around the world, and when this water is dumped the organisms find a new environment in which to take hold. Ships visiting Antarctica are now being asked not to dump their ballast water as it will almost certainly have come from some other ocean.

Bacteria and other small organisms can also be transported unwittingly on the soles of boots and shoes. Recognising this threat, responsible tour operators now require their passengers to disinfect their footwear between landings. This is usually done with physical scrubbing to remove the obvious mud and guano, followed by walking across a mat saturated with a biocide, such as Virkon, which kills microbes.

The harshness of Antarctica's weather has thus far protected it from most alien species, but it is likely the risk of invasion will increase as a consequence of climate change. Warming conditions mean species that are only moderately adapted for cold may have the opportunity to colonise the land and waters of Antarctica.

OZONE DEPLETION

In 1985, the ozone layer above Antarctica was discovered to have thinned so dramatically that it became known as a 'hole' in the ozone. This thinning was caused by human activity, in particular the release of industrial compounds into the atmosphere. The hole increased in size for two decades. Only from 2004 to 2006 did it stop widening.

Ozone is a molecule made up of three oxygen atoms (O_3). It occurs in the stratosphere, between 15 to 40 km (9.3 to 25 miles) above the Earth's surface. Ozone plays a crucial role in filtering out and stopping dangerous ultraviolet radiation (UV-B) from reaching the Earth's surface. UV-B radiation (the major component of sunlight) attacks membranes and DNA in cells, causing mutations and death. Humans living in the southern hemisphere know all too well the damaging effects of an increase in exposure to UV-B radiation. Over the past the 20 years in Australia and New Zealand there have been marked increases in skin cancers, and these have been attributed to the increased size of the ozone hole.

The destruction of ozone is caused by rising levels of chlorine and bromine in the atmosphere. Atmospheric circulation patterns move the polluted air to Antarctica from the industrial northern hemisphere. Chlorofluorocarbons (CFCs) manufactured for use as refrigerants, cleaning agents and aerosol-spray propellants are the main culprit in the chlorine increase; methyl bromine is common in agricultural biocides that kill insect and microbial pests.

During winter, CFCs build up in the atmosphere above Antarctica, and when the first rays of sunlight appear in early spring the hole begins to grow: the sunlight provides the energy needed to start a chemical reaction in which the chlorine atoms in CFCs destroy the ozone molecules. During September, the ozone hole typically reaches its maximum size. It then starts to drift northward through October and November, disappearing from Antarctica in December as atmospheric circulation refills it with ozone from temperate areas. In 2000, the hole was 29 million sq km (11.3 million sq miles) in size.

Recent studies indicate that the ozone hole and resulting increased levels of UV-B are damaging the Antarctic ecosystem. Some species of phytoplankton appear to be particularly susceptible, decreasing productivity by up to 12 percent.

The destruction of the ozone layer has, thankfully, not gone unnoticed by the international community. With such strong evidence pointing to the role of CFCs, an international agreement calling for a phasing-out of the production of CFCs and other ozone-destroying compounds was signed in 1987. This agreement, the Montreal Protocol on Substances that Deplete the Ozone Layer, has been an astounding success in achieving decreased production of CFCs and apparently slowing the growth of the ozone hole.

GLOBAL WARMING

At the beginning of the twenty-first century, climate change became recognised as one of the most serious environmental issues of our time and for the future. It poses the greatest threat to biodiversity in Antarctica and other regions on Earth. Simply put, Antarctica is feeling the heat as a consequence of global climate change and warming. Mean temperatures on the Antarctic Peninsula have increased by 2.5°C (4.5°F) since the 1950s, and in recent years large ice shelves have disintegrated.

To understand this problem it is essential first to examine the potential causes of increases in global temperatures. As we all know, the Earth is warmed by energy from the sun. The Earth's atmosphere acts like the glass in a greenhouse by not only allowing the sun's heat to reach the planet's surface, but also retarding its loss back into space. Some gases, such as carbon dioxide (CO_2) and methane, are particularly adept at trapping heat. The greater the concentration of these 'greenhouse gases', the greater the potential to trap heat and the higher the temperature will rise.

Since the industrial revolution, the CO_2 in the atmosphere has risen dramatically as a consequence of the burning of fossil fuels, and of deforestation, which removes a huge volume of plants that would otherwise be available to absorb and bind CO_2. Direct measurement of the CO_2 level by Mauna Loa observatory in Hawai'i shows that it has increased from about 315 ppm (parts per million) in 1960 to about 375 ppm in 2005, and that the rate is increasing. Antarctica is an important site for monitoring these changes as gases are trapped in ice as it freezes. At Concordia Station, high on the Antarctic ice sheet, cores drilled through the ice cap have provided a plotted history of global carbon dioxide levels and temperatures over the past 650,000 years. Scientists have found that today's concentration of CO_2 is 30 percent higher and rising 200 times faster than at any point in the last 650,000 years.

threats to Antarctica

Collapse of the Larsen B Ice Shelf

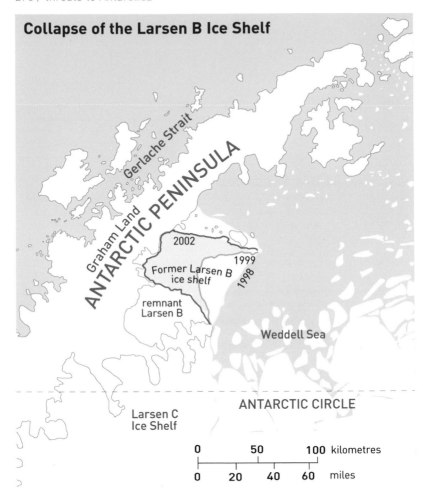

The increase in atmospheric CO_2 translates into an increase in mean global temperature, but this does not mean all places on Earth get hotter. In Antarctica, for instance, temperatures recorded over the past 50 years show that only the Antarctic Peninsula has warmed, while the rest of Antarctica currently shows no sign of rising temperatures. However, in the last 100 years the temperature increase on the Antarctic Peninsula has been two to three times greater than the global average of 0.6°C/1.08°F.

Such increases probably explain the collapse of large ice shelves on the east coast of the peninsula over the past decade. The collapse of the Larsen B ice shelf in early 2002 was the most spectacular (see map opposite). Over a 35-day period, more than 3000 sq km (1875 sq miles) of ice, 200 m (650 ft) thick, broke off and floated out to sea as a flotilla of icebergs.

Since 1974, seven ice shelves have declined in area by a total of about 13,000 sq km (8125 sq miles). Temperature increases also seem responsible for the spread and increasing abundance of the two flowering plants – hairgrass and pearlwort – on the Antarctic Peninsula.

The most serious impact of increasing temperatures is a reduction in krill, the shrimp-like creatures that provide food for many fish, birds and whales. This is occurring because the sea ice, which is an important feeding-ground and nursery for krill in winter, is forming later and retreating earlier, especially around the Antarctic Peninsula and in the south-west Atlantic sector of Antarctica. A survey in this region indicates that krill may have dropped 80 percent in the past 30 years. In an ecosystem where so many animals depend on krill, this could have a serious impact on the Antarctic food web and may explain the decline in some penguin populations.

What does the future hold? Climate change models have been developed to predict temperature rises in the future. Most take into consideration the rising CO_2 emissions as China and India beef up their industries, burning ever more fossil fuel, and the human population continues to grow.

Conservative climate models anticipate a warming of between 1.4°C to 5.8°C (2.5–10.4°F) in mean global temperatures by 2100. Some models, however, predict even greater temperature increases, especially if CO_2 emissions continue to rise at unprecedented rates.

For Antarctica, most models predict only a relatively modest temperature increase across the continent, although if the recent rate of warming in the Antarctic Peninsula is anything to go by, certain regions may see large temperature rises.

threats to Antarctica

CONSERVATION STATUS OF WILDLIFE

In this guide we have used the World Conservation Union (IUCN) Red List of Threatened Species (2010) to indicate the current conservation status of wildlife. The aim of this list is to provide an explicit, objective framework for the classification of species according to their extinction risk. Opposite is a simplified and abbreviated version of the categories and criteria used. The list uses the scientific term 'taxon'. In lay terms, a taxon is simply a group of living or extinct organisms. Further details and information on the outstanding work of IUCN can be found at www.iucn.org and www.iucnredlist.org.

IUCN RED LIST OF THREATENED SPECIES – CATEGORIES AND CRITERIA

Extinct A taxon is Extinct when there is no reasonable doubt that the last individual has died. A taxon is Presumed Extinct when exhaustive surveys in known and/or expected habitat, at appropriate times (diurnal, seasonal, annual) throughout its historic range have failed to record an individual.

Extinct in the Wild A taxon is Extinct in the Wild when it is known only to survive in cultivation, in captivity or as a naturalised population (or populations) well outside the past range.

Critically Endangered A taxon is Critically Endangered when the best available evidence shows that there are fewer than 250 animals, and/or populations have declined or are projected to decline by greater than 80 percent over 10 years, indicating the species to be facing an extremely high risk of extinction in the wild.

Endangered A taxon is Endangered when the best available evidence shows that there are fewer than 2500 animals, and/or populations have declined or are projected to decline by greater than 50 percent over 10 years, indicating the species to be facing a very high risk of extinction in the wild.

Vulnerable A taxon is Vulnerable when the best available evidence shows that there are fewer than 10,000 animals, and/or populations have declined or are projected to decline by greater than 30 percent over 10 years, indicating the species to be facing a high risk of extinction in the wild.

Lower risk A taxon is Lower Risk when it has been evaluated and does not satisfy the criteria for any of the categories Critically Endangered, Endangered or Vulnerable. Taxa included in the Lower Risk Category can be separated into three subcategories:

Conservation Dependent Taxa which are the focus of a continuing taxon-specific or habitat-specific conservation programme targeted towards the taxon in question, the cessation of which would result in the taxon qualifying for one of the threatened categories above within a period of five years.
Near Threatened Taxa which do not qualify for Conservation Dependent, but which are close to qualifying for Vulnerable.
Least Concern Taxa which do not qualify for Conservation Dependent or Near Threatened.

Guidelines for visitors

The Guidance for Visitors to the Antarctic, as set out in Recommendation XVIII-1 of the Antarctic Treaty Consultative Meeting of 1994, are:

PROTECT ANTARCTIC WILDLIFE

Taking or harmful interference with Antarctic wildlife is prohibited except in accordance with a permit issued by a national authority.

1 Do not use aircraft, vessels, small boats or other means of transport in ways that disturb wildlife, either at sea or on land.
2 Do not feed, touch or handle birds or seals, or approach or photograph them in ways that cause them to alter their behavior. Special care is needed when animals are breeding or moulting.
3 Do not damage plants, for example by walking, driving, or landing on extensive moss beds or lichen-covered scree slopes.
4 Do not use guns or explosives. Keep noise to the minimum to avoid frightening wildlife.
5 Do not bring non-native plants or animals into the Antarctic (e.g. live poultry, pet dogs and cats, house plants).

RESPECT PROTECTED AREAS

A variety of areas in the Antarctic have been afforded special protection because of their particular ecological, scientific, historic or other values. Entry into certain areas may be prohibited except in accordance with a permit issued by an appropriate national authority. Activities in and near designated Historic Sites and Monuments and certain other areas may be subject to special restrictions.

1 Know the locations of areas that have been afforded special protection and any restrictions regarding entry and activities that can be carried out in and near them.
2 Observe applicable restrictions.
3 Do not damage, remove or destroy Historic Sites or Monuments, or any artefacts associated with them.

RESPECT SCIENTIFIC RESEARCH

Do not interfere with scientific research, facilities or equipment.

1 Obtain permission before visiting Antarctic science and logistic support facilities; reconfirm arrangements 24 to 72 hours before arriving; and comply strictly with the rules regarding such visits.
2 Do not interfere with, or remove, scientific equipment or marker posts, and do not disturb experimental study sites, field camps or supplies.

BE SAFE

Be prepared for severe and changeable weather. Ensure that your equipment and clothing meet Antarctic standards. Remember that the Antarctic environment is inhospitable, unpredictable and potentially dangerous.

1 Know your capabilities, the dangers posed by the Antarctic environment, and act accordingly. Plan activities with safety in mind at all times.
2 Keep a safe distance from all wildlife, both on land and at sea.
3 Take note of, and act on, the advice and instructions from your leaders; do not stray from your group.
4 Do not walk on to glaciers or large snow fields without proper equipment and experience; there is a real danger of falling into hidden crevasses.
5 Do not expect a rescue service; self-sufficiency is increased and risks reduced by sound planning, quality equipment and trained personnel.
6 Do not enter emergency refuges (except in emergencies). If you use equipment or food from a refuge, inform the nearest research station or national authority once the emergency is over.
7 Respect any smoking restrictions, particularly around buildings, and take great care to safeguard against the danger of fire. This is a real hazard in the dry environment of Antarctica.

KEEP ANTARCTICA PRISTINE

Antarctica remains relatively pristine, and has not yet been subjected to large-scale human perturbations. It is the largest wilderness area on Earth. Please keep it that way.

1 Do not dispose of litter or garbage on land. Open burning is prohibited.
2 Do not disturb or pollute lakes or streams. Any materials discarded at sea must be disposed of properly.
3 Do not paint or engrave names or graffiti on rocks or buildings.
4 Do not collect or take away biological or geological specimens or man-made artefacts as a souvenir, including rocks, bones, eggs, fossils, and parts or contents of buildings.
5 Do not deface or vandalise buildings, whether occupied, abandoned or unoccupied, or emergency refuges.

Wandering albatross

Glossary

Antarctic Circle Line of latitude around the Earth at 66°33'S, where the sun fails to set on the summer solstice (December 21). Locations south of the Antarctic Circle will have days in summer when the sun never sets, and days in winter when the sun never rises.

Antarctic Convergence (Polar Front) Maritime boundary at the northern reaches of the Southern Ocean; occurs between 50°–60°S, where the cold surface water from the Antarctic drops below the warmer northerly waters.

Antarctic Specially Protected Area (ASPA) Area of outstanding wildernesss, scientific or environmental values; a permit is required for entry.

Antarctic Specially Managed Area (ASMA) Area where human activities need to be coordinated and conform to a specific management plan. Deception Island is an example of an ASMA.

baleen Also known as whalebone, baleen are plates of keratinised tissue that hang from the roof of the mouth in some whales. Similar in feel to human fingernails, baleen plates form a filter through which some whales strain krill and fish from the water. Prior to the invention of plastic, baleen was used for items requiring strength and flexibility.

bergy bit Chunk of freshwater ice between 1–5 m (3.2–16.5 ft) in height above sea level; smaller than an iceberg, but bigger than a growler.

biodiversity Numbers of different species of plants and animals within a region.

brash ice Small pieces of ice, less than 2 m (6.5 ft) in diameter, that have broken off icebergs or ice floes.

calving Process by which pieces of ice fall from glaciers or icebergs into the sea.

caldera Large volcanic crater.

CCAMLR Convention on the Conservation of Antarctic Marine Living Resources; enacted in 1982 to protect the seas surrounding Antarctica. (The Antarctic Treaty had not addressed the marine environment.)

circumpolar Around the North Pole or South Pole.

crevasse Crack on the surface of a glacier. Crevasses are usually tens of metres deep and often covered with a thin layer of snow. This makes them difficult to spot and disguises their great danger to people walking on glaciers.

diatom One-celled marine alga with rigid shapes of silica; type of phytoplankton.

ecosystem Complex set of relationships that connect plants, animals and other organisms with one another and with the physical characteristics of the same environment.

Environmental Protocol The Protocol on Environmental Protection to the Antarctic Treaty; agreed in Madrid in 1991 and came into force in 1998. Designates Antarctica 'a natural reserve devoted to peace and science' and bans mining and other exploitation.

fast ice Sea ice that is attached to land, and forms a continuous sheet from the land. Outer regions that break away form pack ice.

firn Granules of compressed snow crystals; an intermediate stage between snow and ice.

fledging Juvenile bird leaving the nest or becoming capable of flight.

floe Piece of floating sea ice. Many floes together make up pack ice.

frazil ice Semi-solid layer of ice, made up of small ice crystals that float near the surface of the sea and have a porridge-like consistency.

grease ice Early stage in the formation of sea ice – a thick layer of ice crystals that have a grease-like appearance.

growler Piece of glacial ice approximately car-size (2–5 m/6.5–16.5 ft in diameter); regarded as smaller than a bergy bit but larger than brash ice. So named because of the sound it makes when scraping along the side of a wooden ship.

gyre Circular current.

Historic Sites and Monuments (HSMs) Historic places and structures protected under the Antarctic Treaty.

iceberg Large piece of floating (or grounded) ice formed from fresh water that has originated from an ice sheet or glacier.

ice core Cylindrical sample of ice obtained from drilling through an ice sheet. Much can be learned about past climatic conditions by studying the gases trapped within the ice of these cores.

ice-edge Border between fast sea ice and open water.

ice shelf Large floating extension of an ice sheet or many glaciers, formed where these flow off the edge of the continent but do not break off at the shore. Often formed in large bays where many glaciers may merge.

IUCN The International Union for the Conservation of Nature; also known as the World Conservation Union.

IWC International Whaling Commission, established in 1946 to regulate whaling for the preservation of the industry. The IWC was not set up to protect whales from hunting, but from over-hunting.

katabatic winds Gravity-driven winds caused by the movement of dense, cold air down slopes from the polar plateau; can reach hurricane force.

keratin Large protein that is the main component of baleen. Also found in skin, hair, fingernails and rhinoceros horns.

krill Small shrimp-like crustacean, of which huge populations occur in the Southern Ocean. Ecological drivers of the Antarctic food web.

lichens Symbiotic organism in which an alga and a fungus cohabit the same structure for the benefit of both. The alga produces food through photosynthesis, and the fungus provides an anchoring body, plus some minerals from the rock on which it lives.

Madrid Protocol *see* Environmental Protocol

mollymawks Old mariner's term for albatrosses; still used today in some countries as a synonym for the smaller albatross species.

Montreal Protocol International agreement regulating the production of chlorofluorocarbons (CFCs) and other ozone-damaging gases.

nunatak Rocky outcrop that pierces and is encircled by an ice sheet.

ornithogenic Coming from or produced by birds.

ozone Three oxygen atoms, O_3, ('regular' oxygen, O_2, has only two atoms) that occurs as a layer in the stratosphere (15–40 km/9.3–25 miles above the surface of the Earth); important in absorbing harmful ultraviolet radiation (UV).

pack ice Sea ice that has broken away from fast sea ice and occurs in consolidated floes; moves about according to winds and currents.

pancake ice Early stage in the formation of sea ice, when grease ice is consolidated into lily-pad or pancake-shaped discs of slush. The edges are raised from bumping into other pancakes.

polynya Area of open water among sea ice, created by a combination of the upwelling of deep, relatively warmer water, and persistent winds or currents. Katabatic winds are important in their formation. Highly productive areas important for marine life.

pressure ridges Ridges of sea ice formed by the action of ice pushing against land or other ice

phytoplankton Any species of plant (phyto) that does not swim on its own power, but instead drifts with the current.

plankton Any animal or plant that does not swim on its own power, but instead drifts with the current. Some species are part of the plankton when eggs or larvae, but free-swimming as adults.

Polar Front *see* Antarctic Convergence.

raft Large collection of sea birds gathered at sea.

rookery Breeding colony of penguins or other sea birds. Also sometimes used to refer to a breeding colony of fur seals or sea lions.

sea ice Any ice formed from the freezing of the surface waters of the sea.

South Geographic Pole Southernmost point on Earth; the axis on which the world rotates.

South Geomagnetic Pole Usually of interest only to geophysists, this would be the location of the end of the magnetic field if the Earth's core were a simple dipolar magnet, like a bar magnet. The Geomagnetic Pole is where the magnetic lines should enter the Earth; the Magnetic Pole is where they actually do.

South Magnetic Pole Pole of the Earth's magnetic field where the lines of the Earth's magnetic field align vertically and enter the Earth; compasses point to the magnetic, not geographic, poles. The magnetic poles are not fixed at a geographical location, but 'wander' over time. When first discovered in 1908, the South Magnetic Pole was in northern Victoria Land, the area of Antarctica south of New Zealand. It is now well offshore in the Ross Sea.

South Pole *see* South Geographic Pole; South Magnetic Pole; South Geomagnetic Pole.

Southern Ocean The southern portions of the Pacific, Atlantic and Indian Oceans and their tributary seas surrounding Antarctica.

tabular iceberg Iceberg with a flat, table-like top. Originating only from ice shelves, tabular bergs are the largest icebergs in the world, with some measuring more than 100 km (62 miles) in length.

taxon Group of related organisms. Examples of taxa include species (for example, Adélie penguin); families (for example, all penguins); classes (for example, all birds).

Photograph credits

All photographs © Peter Carey & Craig Franklin, except as follows (copyright © as credited):

INTRODUCING ANTARCTICA
page 21, Amundsen-Scott South Pole Station: National Science Foundation/United States Antarctic Program

PLACES
page 88, Neko Harbour (top): Shaun Powell
page 90, Petermann Island (top): John Bowers

LIFE IN ANTARCTICA
page 147, krill, Robert King, AAD/Commonwealth of Australia

BIRDS
page 150–52, Light-mantled sooty albatross: John Bowers
page 156, Black-browed albatross: John Bowers
page 157, Royal albatross: Nadine Gibbs
page 160, Grey-headed albatross (bottom): Melanie Powell
page 163, Light-mantled sooty albatross: John Bowers
page 172, Snow petrel pair (top): Robert Suisted, www.naturespic.com
page 176, White-chinned petrel (top): Mark Fraser
page 178, Wilson's storm petrel: Mark Hannaford
page 180, Sooty shearwater (top): Brent Stephenson @ Eco-Vista; (bottom): Paul Sagar
page 192, Antarctic tern: John Bowers

MAMMALS
page 238, Ross seal (top): John Bowers; (bottom): Bruce Dix, New Zealand Department of Conservation
page 242, Humpback whale: Hedgehog House
page 245, Blue whale (bottom right): Hedgehog House
page 246, Blue whale: Nadine Gibbs
page 250, Blue whale: Nadine Gibbs
page 252, Fin whale: Gerhard Hüdepohl, www.atacamaphoto.com
page 254, Humpback whale (bottom): John Bowers
page 256, Killer whales (bottom): Darrel Day/*Spirit of Sydney*
page 258, Minke whales (bottom): Hedgehog House

BACK COVER
Antarctic tern: John Bowers

Acknowledgements

As with any book that is built on years of experiences, this book could not have happened without assistance from a wide variety of people. We travelled to Antarctica with the New Zealand Antarctic Research Programme (and its many newer incarnations) and the Australian National Antarctic Research Expedition, and on cruise ships operated by Abercrombie & Kent, Crystal Cruises, Lindblad Expeditions, Orient Lines, Salen-Lindblad, Seaquest Cruises, TCS Expeditions, and Voyages of Discovery. Every trip to the far south reveals something new and we are grateful to have had the opportunity, since 1986, to work in the most beautiful place on the planet.

Thanks to Noel Miller, Paul Sagar, Sean Fitzsimons and Gabriela Roldan for critical comments on the manuscript, and to Russell Thompson for tracking down the true identity of Una. Peter Cleary and Malcolm Macfarlane were both generous in sharing with us their encyclopaedic knowledge of the Antarctic. We thank Colin Miskelly for ferreting out typos and errors with his thorough proofreading. Thanks to Debbie Summers for help with Falkland

Islands information, and Phil Lyver and David Ainley for sharing their knowledge of Adélie penguin population trends in the Ross Sea. Neil Gilbert and Antarctica New Zealand generously allowed us to use their maps of the historic hut areas at Capes Adare and Evans. Tourist statistics are courtesy of the International Association of Antarctica Tour Operators. We thank John Bowers, Darrel Day, Mark Fraser, Nadine Gibbs, Mark Hannaford, Gerhard Hüdepohl, Robert King, Colin Miskelly, Melanie Powell, Shaun Powell, Paul Sagar and Richard White for generously allowing us to use their photographs. Sarah Bennett and Mary Varnham of Awa Press provided many ideas to help shape the finished product, and we are grateful for their considerable input.

A special mention is also due to Bill Davison, an outstanding Antarctic scientist who kindly included us as his research slaves in the 1980s and who thus launched our Antarctic careers. Cheers, Bill.

Peter Carey & Craig Franklin

Index

Adams, Jameson, 105
Adélie penguin, 202–203
  largest colony (worldwide), 97, 99
Admiralty Bay, King George Island, 55
airstrip, King George Island, 55
Aitcho Islands, 61
albatrosses, 154, 158–67
Albert Crary Laboratory, 109
algae, 91, 137–39
Almirante Brown, *see* Brown Station
Amundsen, Roald, 93
Andvord Bay, 89
Antarctic Circle, 279
Antarctic Coastal Current, 142
Antarctic Convergence, 7, 29, 141–42, 279
Antarctic fur seal, 230–31
Antarctic Heritage Trust, 103, 111
Antarctic Peninsula, 62–93, 138
  map, ii
Antarctic petrel, 168–69
Antarctic prion, 184–85
Antarctic shag, 155, 156, 186–87
Antarctic (ship), 65, 71
Antarctic Sound, 65
Antarctic Specially Managed Area (ASMA), 279
Antarctic Specially Protected Area (ASPA), 279
Antarctic tern, 192–93
Antarctic toothfish, 266
Antarctic Treaty, 7, 21–23, 239, 262, 275
anti-freeze, 140, 149
Anvers Island, 83, 93
Arctowski, Henryk, 57
Arctowski Station, King George Island, 57
Argentina, *see* Ushuaia

Argentine bases
  Deception Island, 35–37
  Half Moon Island, 47–49
  Hope Bay, 66–67
  King George Island, 54–55
  Paradise Harbour, 74–81
Aurora (ship), 103

Bagshawe, Thomas, 77
Baily Head, Deception Island, 42–43
baleen whales, 249–53, 256–59, 279
Bay of Whales, 113
Beagle Channel, 27
Belgica expedition (1897–99), 57, 73, 83, 93
bergy bits, 16, 17, 279
birds, 150–221
  behaviour, 155–56
  body form, 154–55
  identification, 157
black-browed albatross, 156, 158–59
blow-holes, 244–45
blue whale, 246, 250–51
Booth Island, 85
Borchgrevink, Carsten, 97, 99
de Bouganville, Louis-Antoine, 121
Brabant Island, 93
Bransfield House, *see* British Base A
Bransfield Strait, 30
brash ice, 17, 279
British Antarctic (*Southern Cross*) Expedition (1899), 97, 99
British Antarctic (*Nimrod*) Expedition (1907–09), 105, 111
British Antarctic Survey, 91
British bases, A, 87
  B, 39, 40
  D, 47

brood patch (penguins), 198
Brown Bluff, 69
Brown Station, Paradise Harbour, 80–81
Bryde Island, 75

caldera, 35, 279
calving, 279
Cámara Station, 49
Cape Adare, 96–99
    map, 98
Cape Evans, 101–103
    map, 102
Cape Horn, 29
Cape petrel, 170–71
cetaceans, 242–59
Charcot, Jean-Baptiste, 91
Chilean bases
    Deception Island, 34–35, 37, 38–39,
       42–43, 44–45
    King George Island, 54–57
    Waterboat Point, 76–77
Chilean sea bass, *see* Patagonian toothfish
chinstrap penguin, 197, 199, 206–207
Circumpolar Current, 29, 142
    map, 142
collembola, 140
Commission for the Conservation of
 Antarctic Marine Living Resources
 (CCAMLR), 262, 266, 279
conservation, of Antarctica, 262–77
    Antarctic Treaty, 7, 21–23, 239, 262
    IUCN Red List of Threatened
       Species, 263, 265, 272–73
Cook, Frederick, 93
Cook, James, 127
cormorants, 118, 119, 155, 186–87
crabeater seal, 143, 225, 232–23
crested penguins, 201, 216–19

crevasse, 279
Cry Of The Penguins, 67
Cuverville Island, 72–73

Dallmann, Eduard, 83, 85, 91
David, John, 121
Deception Island, 34–45
    map, iv
diatom, 280
dinoflagellates, 106
Discovery expedition (1901–04), 101, 111
Discovery Hut, 111
Doumer Island, 83
Drake Passage, 9, 28–29, 116
Drygalski Fiord, 126
Dundee Island, 65

eared seals, 229
East Antarctica, 9, 13
ecosystem, marine, 141–49
ecosystem, terrestrial, 137–40
elephant seal, 236–237
Elephant Island, 129, 130
    see also Point Wild
emperor penguin, 199, 200, 208–209
Endurance expedition (1914–16), 33, 129
Environmental Protocol (Madrid),
 262, 280
Erebus (ship), 94
Esperanza station, 66–67
Euphausia superba, 147
Evans, Edward, 101
expeditions
    Belgica (1897–99), 57, 73, 83, 93
    British Antarctic (*Southern Cross*)
       (1899), 97, 99
    British Antarctic (*Nimrod*) (1907–09),
       105, 111

expeditions *continued*
   Discovery (1901–04), 101, 111
   Endurance (1914–16), 33
   Imperial Trans-Antarctic (1914–17),
     101–102, 105, 111, 129
   Polar Shipping Corporation
     (*Polarschiffahrtsgesellschaft*) (1874), 83
   Quest (1921–22), 129
   Swedish Antarctic (1901–03), 65, 66,
     67, 71
   Terra Nova (1910–13), 97, 101, 111

Falkland Islands, 114–23
   Dependencies Survey, 85
   map, vii
False Cape Renard, 85
fast ice, 19, 280
feathers, 197
Fief Mountains, 87
fin whale, 252–53
firn, 11, 280
fish, 149
fishing, 266
floe, 280
flukes, 244
food web, 144–45
Fortuna Bay, 130
frazil ice, 19, 280
fulmar, southern, *see* southern fulmar
fur seal, *see* Antarctic fur seal

gentoo penguin, 196, 199, 201, 214–15
geology, 20
geothermal hot springs, 35
Gypsy Cove, 117
de Gerlache, Adrien, 57, 73, 83, 93
Gerlache Strait, 92–93
   map, iii
giant petrel, *see* Southern giant petrel
glacier, 10–16
glacier ice, 15
global warming, 62, 263, 269–71
Gold Harbour, 132

Gondwana, 8–9, 116
Gonzalez Videla Station, Waterboat
  Point, 76, 77
graves, 39
   Nicolai Hanson, 99
   Ernest Shackleton, 129, 131
   Ole Wennersgaard, 71
grease ice, 280
Greenpeace, 103
greenhouse effect, 69–71
Greenwich Island, 58–59
grey-headed albatross, 160–61
growler, 17, 280
Grytviken, 128, 130, 131
guidelines for visitors, 275–77
gull, kelp, 188–89
gyre, 280

hair grass, 139
Half Moon Island, 20, 46–49
Hannah Point, Livingston Island, 50–53
Hanson, Nicolai (grave), 99
Hayward, V.G., 103
Hektor whaling station, 39
Herring, Joseph, 55
Historic Sites and Monuments (HSM;
  designated), 41, 45, 67, 71, 91, 97, 101,
  103, 111, 280
Hope Bay, 66–67
hotsprings, 35
humpback whale, 242, 247, 254–55
huts
   Cape Adare (Borchgrevink), 96, 97
   Cape Evans (Scott), 101–103
   Cape Royds (Shackleton), 104–106
   Hope Bay, 66, 67
   McMurdo (Discovery), 110, 111
   Paulet Island (Larsen's), 70, 71
   Waterboat Point, 76, 77

ice core, 280
ice-edge, 280
ice sheet, 12–15

ice shelf, 14, 280
icebergs, 14–17, 65, 280
icefish, 149
Imperial Trans-Antarctic Expedition
  (1914–17), 101–102, 105, 111, 129
In the Footsteps of Scott (expedition),
  103
insects, 140
International Whaling Commission
  (IWC), 265, 281
Isla San Pedro, *see* South Georgia
Islas Malvinas, *see* Falkland Islands
IUCN (World Conservation Union) Red
  List of Threatened Species, 263, 265,
  272–73, 281

jellyfish, 146
Joinville Island, 65
Jougla Point, 87
Jun, Jaegyu, 65

katabatic winds, 65, 281
keratin, 281
kelp gull, 188–89
killer whale, 201, 256–57
King Edward Point, 130
King George Island, 54–55
king penguin, 210–13
krill, 136, 147, 281

Larsen, Carl, 71, 128
Larsen B ice shelf, 270–71
latitude, 10
Lemaire Channel, 84–85
Lemaire Island, 75
leopard seal, 234–35
Lester, Maxime Charles, 77
leucistic (white) penguins, 79
lichens, 37, 47, 57, 59, 61, 139, 72–73
  139, 281
light-mantled sooty albatross, 150, 162–63
limpets, 148
Livingston Island, 47, 50–53

macaroni penguin, 201, 216–17
Mackintosh, Aeneas, 103
Madrid Environmental Protocol, *see*
  Environmental Protocol
Magellanic penguin, 220–21
Mahu, Jacob, 30
mammals, 222–59
maps
  Antarctica, i
  Antarctic Peninsula, ii
  Cape Adare, 98
  Cape Evans, 102
  Circumpolar Current, 142
  Gerlache Strait, iii
  Deception Island, iv
  Falkland Islands, vii
  Larsen B ice shelf, 270
  Ross Island, vi
  Ross Sea, v
  South Georgia, vii
  South Shetland Islands, iv
marine food web, 144–45
Marshall, Eric, 105
Maxwell Bay, King George Island, 55
McMurdo Sound, 101
McMurdo Station, 108–11
Megalestris Hill, 91
minerals, 20
minke whale, 245, 258–59
mites, 140
mollymawks, 281
Montreal Protocol, 281
monuments, *see* Historic Sites and
  Monuments
mosses, 45, 59, 73, 138, 139
moulting, feathers, 198
Mount Pond, 35
Mr Forbush And The Penguins, 67

Neko Harbour, 88–89
Neptune's Bellows, 34, 36, 37, 38, 39
Neptune's Window, 39, 41
Neumayer Channel, 82–83

Nimrod, 105, 111
von Neumayer, Georg, 83
Nordenskjöld, Otto, 65, 67, 71
nunatak, 281

Operation Tabarin, 39, 87
orca, *see* killer whale
ozone, 268, 281
   depletion, 267–69

pack ice, 19
Palmer Station, 81
pancake ice, 18, 19, 281
Paradise Harbour, 74–75
Pardo, Luis (bust), 32, 33
Patagonian toothfish (Chilean sea bass), 266
Paulet Island, 70–71
pearlwort, 139
Pendulum Cove, Deception Island, 44–45
penguins, 196–221
   behaviour, 199
   body form, 197–98
   identification, 200–201
Petermann Island, 90–91
petrels, 168–83
phocid seals, 229
photosynthesis, 146
phytoplankton, 144–47, 281
Piloto Pardo, 35, 45
pipit, South Georgia, 126
pintail, South Georgia, 126
plankton, 146–47, 281
plant life, 138–39
Point Wild, Elephant Island, 32–33
Polar Front, *see* Antarctic Convergence
Polar Plateau, 12
Polar Shipping Corporation
   (*Polarschiffahrtsgesellschaft*) expedition
   (1874), 83, 91
Polish base, Arctowski Station, 56–57
political Antarctica, 21–23
polynya, 143, 281

Port Circumcision, 91
Port Foster, 35
Port Lockroy, 87
Port Louis, 121, 123
precipitation, 11, 12–13
Presidente Pedro Augirre Cerda
   (Chilean base), 45
pressure ridges, 281
prion, *see* Antarctic prion
Prion Island, 132

Quest expedition (1921–22), 129

Rancho Point, Deception Island, 43
Ridley Beach, 99
de la Roché, Antoine, 127
rockhopper penguin, 218–19
Rongé Island, 73
Ross Ice Shelf, 112–13
Ross Island, 96–111
   map, vi
Ross, James, 94, 99, 113
Ross Sea, 94–113
   map, v
Ross seal, 238–39
Royal Bay, 132
Royds, Charles, 105
royal albatross, 157, 164–65

Salisbury Plain, 132
salt glands, 153
San Telmo, 53
Scott Base, 109, 111
Scott, Robert (Falcon), 97, 98, 103, 111
sea birds, 152–95
sea ice, 18–19, 143, 147
Sea Lion Island, 118, 121
sea spiders, 148
sealing, 55, 83, 127–29, 264
seals, 224–41
   behaviour, 226–27
   body form, 226
   breeding, 227–28

identification, 228–29
Shackleton, Ernest, 33, 105, 111, 129, 131
shag, Antarctic, *see* Antarctic Shag
shearwater, sooty, 180–81
skua, 190–91
Smith, William, 30, 55
snow algae, 138
snow petrel, 172–73
snowy sheathbill, 194–95
sooty shearwater, 180–81
South Georgia, 124–33, 129
    map, vii
South Pole, 10, 21, 282
South Sandwich Islands, 130
South Shetland Islands, 30–61, 138
    map, iv
Southern Cross, 97
southern elephant seal, 224, 236–37
southern fulmar, 182–83
southern giant petrel, 144, 174–75
Southern Ocean, 6, 7, 141–43, 265
Spencer-Smith, Arnold, 103
springtails, 140
squid, 149
Stanley, 85, 130
starfish, 148
storm petrel, Wilson's, 178–79
Stromness (whaling station), 130
St Andrews Bay, 132
Swedish Antarctic Expedition (1901–03), 65, 66, 67, 71
swimming, 41, 45

tardigrades, 140
tern, Antarctic, *see* Antarctic tern
Terra Nova expedition (1910–13), 97, 101, 111
terrestrial ecosystem, 137–40
territorial claims, 21–23
Terror (ship), 94
toothed whales, 245, 248
Transantarctic Mountain Range, 9

Trinity House, *see* British Base D
tube-noses, 154

Una's Tits, 85
United Kingdom bases, *see* British Bases
Ushuaia, 26–27

Vince, George, 111
visitors' guidelines, 275–77
volcanic eruption, 39, 45
volcanic islands, 34–41, 70–71

Wandel Peak, 85
wandering albatross, 166–67
Waterboat Point, Paradise Harbour, 76–79
Weddell Sea, 62, 65, 71, 77
Weddell seal, 228, 240–41
Wennersgaard, Ole, 71
West Antarctica, 9, 13
Whaler's Bay, Deception Island, 38–41
whales, 242–59
    behaviour, 247
    body form, 244–46
    bones, 57, 61, 87
    identification, 248–49
whaling, 39, 89, 128–29, 265
    station, 39, 87, 128–29, 130
white-chinned petrel, 176–77
Wiencke Island, 83, 87
Wild, Frank, 33, 105
Wilson's storm petrel, 178–79
World Conservation Union, *see* IUCN
worm, nematode, 140
    marine, 148
Worsley, Frank, 129

Yahgan Indians, 27, 121
Yankee Harbour, Greenwich Island, 58–59
Yelcho, 33

zooplankton, 146–47

EXPLORE THE WORLD WITH AWA PRESS

The Miss Tutti Frutti Contest
Graeme Lay
Savour the South Pacific islands – sublimely beautiful, blissfully remote, and long the haven of artists and writers seeking an earthly paradise.

An Afternoon in Summer
Kathy Giuffre
Experience a year in the South Seas with an American woman who escapes life's stresses by taking her young sons to live on a tropical island.

Embracing the Dragon
Polly Greeks
Trek on the Great Wall of China in this unputdownable story of a woman's quest for love and adventure on China's ancient frontier.

The Torchlight List
Jim Flynn
Join an inspirational professor as he travels around the world of books. Read, learn, and discover the magic realm of knowledge and imagination.

How to Gaze at the Southern Stars
Richard Hall
Explore the heavens with a remarkable astronomer as he blends startling discoveries of modern science with stories of how early civilisations lived by the stars.

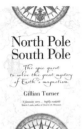

North Pole, South Pole
Gillian Turner
Take an imaginary trip inside the Earth to find the source of our planet's amazing magnetic field.

AVAILABLE FROM BOOKSTORES, OR PURCHASE ONLINE AT www.awapress.com.

Awa Press
PO Box 11-416, Wellington 6142, New Zealand
tel +64 4 385 0740 fax +64 4 382 9032
All our books may be purchased for retail, corporate gifts and special promotions at discount rates. Contact **sales@awapress.com** for details.